FALLING IN LOVE
WITH YOUR

Hans Schumann

Published by Hans Schumann Coaching Limited.

Copyright © 2016 by Hans Schumann Coaching Limited.

ISBN-13: 978-1540351142
ISBN-10: 1540351149

Neither the publisher nor the author is engaged in rendering professional or personal services or advice to the individual reader. The ideas, procedures and suggestions contained in this book are not intended as a substitute for consulting with a career advisor, therapist or physician. All matters regarding your mental or physical wellbeing require attention by a physician or therapist. Neither the author not the publisher shall be liable or responsible for any loss or damage allegedly arising from any information or suggestion in this book. The intent of the author is only to offer information of a general nature to help readers in their quest for job satisfaction.

This book contains case studies of real people, included with their permission. Their names, industries and sometimes gender have been changed to protect confidentiality.

"Masterful Living" is registered in the United Kingdom as a trademark of Hans Schumann Coaching Limited. All rights reserved.

"The Dream Job Formula" is an unregistered trademark of Hans Schumann Coaching Limited. All rights reserved.

Book cover by Daliborka Mijailovic.

"A must-have for those considering a change in career or even for those wanting to rediscover their passion for their current role. Written with the empathy and courage of personal experience, and the rich diversity of others' perspectives, to create a compelling and thought-provoking message for the reflective and conscientious professional."

- Jess Petrie, Lawyer, Financial Services

"Refreshing and written wonderfully clearly! Everything is presented aptly and to the point, well analysed and succinct. It's been a pleasure to read this book. Going through all the exercises has greatly increased my quality of life. Thank you! The learnings are also transferable to other areas of life that are not fully balanced. Hans Schumann opens doors for everybody, whatever their problem. It's a gift!"

- Anja Biewer, Civil Judge, Regional Court, Germany

"This book is packed with useful exercises all relevant and easy to use with illustrative case studies throughout. It deals with all the objections we might have to moving forward and the result is a work of real humanity and understanding of just how challenging this process can be. This is an excellent self-help book and deserves to be widely read – highly recommended."

- Ross Nichols, The Transition Transformer™, Business Mentor, Coach, Contrarian and Speaker

"Whether you are hitting a career crisis or considering changing your work or nature of job, you will find this book invaluable to help you along establishing that change. This book is for anyone considering a change in their work and wanting to pinpoint what's next. It's a must-read and I highly recommend this book."

- Rafah Sabbagh, Coach, Wellness Consultant, Speaker & Writer

Contents

Acknowledgements

I am the sum of the people I have encountered throughout my life:

- those who nurtured and taught me;
- those who loved or hurt me; and
- those who supported or challenged me.

Each encounter has changed my life and they were all important for my personal growth. They eventually led me to write this book.

I would not be where I am now without my parents, who have loved and nurtured me all through my life. They also gave me opportunities for growth and development for which I am eternally grateful.

I would never have moved to London if it had not been for my ex-partner Derek Smith, whom I thank for some of the best years in my life.

I probably would not have found a job in London if it had not been for Mark Lubbock, who changed my life by giving me a top job in the City at a time when I encountered closed doors everywhere else.

I might not have overcome my health crisis without the assistance of my A-Team of health practitioners who supported me through two years of serious illness: Dr Robert Logan, Jane Wilson, Jackie Hales, Andrea Walker, Lucia Nella, Jordan Reasoner, Steve Wright, Dr Nilesh Wadke and Dr Jens Rohrbeck.

I might still be lost and depressed without the support of my own coach, teacher and mentor Tony J Selimi, who was instrumental in rebuilding my life from the ashes.

I might never have left the legal profession to become a life coach if I had not found the Demartini Value Determination Process®. I would like to thank Dr John Demartini for his profound life's work and also for giving me permission to include his process in this book.

Special thanks also go to the following people:

My sister, who holds our family together like a lioness and from whom I learn so much about myself.

Hendrik Backerra, my best friend and a masterful corporate coach and trainer. He has been a loving constant in my life since I was 10 years old. A rock of loyalty and love, even at those times when I had little of that to give myself.

Jill Bohnhorst, my chosen sister and guardian angel, who makes me laugh like no one else.

My friends who nurtured and supported me during my years of illness: Derek Smith, Bassam Al Tamimi, David Sorsoli, David Hedges, Jeffrey and Tibor Kiser-Paradi, Carmen Deans, Richard Saunders, Martin Moody, Ben Collins and Stephen Pelton.

Ashley Lloyd Shaw, who sent me a message at a low point in my life that brought me back on my path.

Nick Bolton for creating the Animas Centre of Coaching, the amazing school that taught me coaching and so much more. He also created the loving and supporting community of coaches that is the backbone of my coaching business.

The members of the Animas Coach Success Programme, who supported me with love, challenge and company.

My amazing clients who inspire and give me purpose in life. I feel honoured by their trust and grateful for the opportunity to learn and grow with them.

Thomas Diekmann, who gave me my first career opportunity and set me up for life by stretching me far outside my comfort zone.

Joanna Day, who gave me fantastic career opportunities in financial services and taught me how to lead with heart and vision.

Dr Voice, who taught me the basics of public speaking and stage presence.

Robert Stephenson, who coached me in preparation of my first motivational speech.

The support team behind my coaching business who bring a magic touch to everything I create: Liz Mattson, Jill Boniface and Chaten Parmer.

Anja Biewer, whose friendship is one of the constants in my life that keep me grounded.

My Reiki teacher Torsten Lange, who connected me with an energy I did not even know I had.

The first reviewers of my book: Anja Biewer, Jill Bohnhorst, Will Harvey, Jessica Petrie, Ross Nichols, Rafah Sabbagh and Chanchala Unantenne.

Thank you!

About the Author

Hans Schumann is a transformational coach with a background in law and financial services going back 20 years. Having seen the benefits of coaching in his own life, he now helps his clients to create life outcomes and manage life challenges more effectively, with a focus on their career decisions, business start-ups and life planning.

His action-orientated coaching process combines tools, processes and models from world-renowned coaching experts with his own experience of overcoming years of struggle. He explores with his clients what really matters to them and helps them lay the foundations for living an inspired and fulfilled life. He calls this process "Masterful Living®".

Hans was born in Hamburg, Germany, where he obtained his first two law degrees and a PhD. He also holds a Master in Law from Queen Mary University, London. For 20 years Hans was working in the legal profession in London, first in private practice and then in financial services. After a serious health crisis lasting two years, which he finally overcame by activating the healing resources of his mind, Hans re-evaluated his life with the tools set out in this book. He then decided to become a personal coach.

Hans is accredited as a coach by the International Coach Federation (ICF) and as a NLP Practitioner by The Association for Neuro-Linguistic Programming (ANLP). He works with a small group of private clients who feel passionate about improving their life mastery. Coaching sessions take place either in London or via Skype. Subject to special arrangements, Hans also travels to other countries to hold workshops or personal coaching sessions.

For feedback, questions or private consultations:

Email Hans at **info@hansschumann.com** or contact him on the
following social networks:

Facebook: https://www.facebook.com/hansschumanncoaching

Twitter: https://twitter.com/lovecreategrow

LinkedIn: https://uk.linkedin.com/in/hansschumann

Foreword

If you have picked up this book, chances are that your work life is not currently a true reflection of your highest personal values. The good news is that you can bring the two into alignment, and this book will show you how. Clearly, simply and meaningfully, it will guide you through the necessary steps to lift your personal and professional success to a new level.

This book is for you if you are struggling to find meaning in a job you do not enjoy. It could be that you are simply working against your natural flow and have lost track of what is really important to you beyond the immediate financial gains. Hans Schumann describes the basic principle that your life must be aligned with your highest personal values. Not only did he learn this the hard way, but he also used his hard-won knowledge to successfully transform his own life, using the tools you will find in this book.

Hans makes no assumptions about who you are or what your options might be. Here you will not find any high-handed rebuke for being out of step with your true self, nor any unrealistic conjecture about throwing it all in and reinventing yourself. Hans understands the realities and pressures of modern life, family responsibilities and financial stability, and accepts that 'for some people, simplicity, predictability and security are enough'.

However, he does not accept that anyone should simply put up with being miserable at work and insists that, in any job, there can be 'a thread of purpose and inspiration that runs through your career and brings a sense of fulfilment that transcends the temporary ups and downs'.

Thus six chapters in this book are devoted to 'Falling in love with your current job'. For those who desire a more radical change, there are also seven chapters on 'Finding a new job'.

Whether you stay where you are or move elsewhere in your career, this book provides you with the key to finding your own personal 'thread of purpose and inspiration' in four main steps: determining your values; creating your personal mission statement; defining your desired life outcomes, and improving your self-management.

What makes this book stand out is its strong focus on our responsibility for our own job satisfaction. Rather than focusing on external factors for stress and motivation, which are often outside our control, the book outlines the many options we have for managing the intrinsic factors. This effective self-management approach is the bedrock of Hans's coaching process, called 'Masterful Living', already described in his e-book, *The 10 Basics of Masterful Living* (a free download at **www.LoveYourJobBook.com**).

Written in a compassionate coaching voice, this book will support you in creating the life you want by asking you powerful questions, challenging you and helping you generate new ideas and options. Hans shares his wisdom in a direct, accessible and non-judgmental way that honours your own values.

This truly is a book for everyone – whether you are boldly striving for a radical new start in life, or simply seeking more contentment in your current situation, there is a wealth of wisdom and inspiration between the covers of this book.

Raymond Aaron

Part 1

Introduction

In this part of the book:

- ✓ We explore what your job means to you
- ✓ We ask whether people ever love their jobs
- ✓ You find out who this book is for
- ✓ You learn the story of my own career change

Chapter 1

What place does your job have in your life?

How do you feel when your alarm rings on a Monday morning? Do you press the snooze button and curse the cruelty of life that forces you to drag yourself back to work? Do you need a coffee and a sugary snack to comfort you and pick you up before you can face the reality of work once again?

I hope you don't! Life is too short to waste it working in a job that you do not enjoy. Work can be an enjoyable part of life and this book will show you how.

The fact that you are holding this book in your hands tells me that you are already thinking about taking steps to improve your satisfaction with your job. Are you maybe:

- looking for a new job?
- considering a change in career?
- wanting to engage with your current job more positively?
- interested in improving your self-management at work?
- looking for a better balance in life?
- seeking to motivate the people who work for you?

Wherever you are on this spectrum, this book will provide you with guidance and inspiration that will help you fall in love with your job. For some of you this may be first love; for others, falling in love again. By this I mean much more than just increasing your job satisfaction. I am encouraging you to find your purpose in life and create fulfilment in your career.

Impossible, you say? Well, I take on the challenge!

I have seen work life from many angles: I have worked in a butcher's shop, at McDonalds, in the German Navy, as a lawyer, in financial services and now as a transformational career and life coach. In this book I am going to share with you what I have learned about job satisfaction and fulfilment, both from my own experience and from observing others. I will introduce you to the simple and effective concepts and tools that fundamentally transformed my own career and brought a fresh sense of fulfilment to my life. They have worked for me and my coaching clients - and they will work for you too!

The essence of this book can be summarised as follow:

Job satisfaction is not something that is given to us. We create it.

We create it either on our own or together with our employer, if we have one. People often overlook the fact that job satisfaction is a shared responsibility, and mainly focus on the actions that their employer should be taking to keep them happy. Human resources departments spend a lot of time and money on staff benefits and engagement programmes, but my experience is that all these efforts have limited effect if employees do not accept their part. You cannot motivate staff if they simply do not *want* to care about their jobs.

How much do **you** care about your job?

During my time in employment, I encountered a lot of complaints from staff, ranging from significant issues such as bullying and burnout down to trivial things like the absence of milk in the kitchen. If you find yourself complaining about your work a lot, you will have to ask yourself what you want to do about it.

Whilst there are only limited ways in which you can influence your employer, you are in full control over the way you show up at work and respond to your environment. You are also free in your decision to leave or stay. Sometimes it may not seem like you have this freedom; for example, if you depend on the money and have no alternative job offers. Yet often this is just an excuse for not moving out of your comfort zone; and growth only happens *outside* the comfort zone.

If it is indeed an existential necessity for you to stay in your current job, then it may be time to appreciate how much you value the security it offers. You can then be grateful that, for the time being, your job pays your bills even if it has its disadvantages.

I am hoping, though, that this book will motivate you to aim for more: to either fall in love with your current job or find a new one that feels inspiring and exciting to you.

Chapter 2

Do people ever love their jobs?

At this point I often hear two objections:

"A dream job is an unattainable fantasy"

When people say this, they usually mean that every job becomes a dire routine after a while. Work is work and as such it is different from pleasure. They believe it is unrealistic to aim for the ideal of a job you love so much that you cannot wait to get up in the morning to go to work.

I agree that work is never just pleasure. A job that is just fun without pain and struggle is indeed a fantasy and that's not what this book is about. I acknowledge that every aspect of life has its ups and downs, rewards and challenges. This includes your career and day-to-day job.

However, there can be a thread of purpose and inspiration that runs through your career and brings a sense of fulfilment that transcends the temporary ups and downs. If you feel truly inspired by your job, you will appreciate the challenges it provides, and you will be better equipped to manage the inevitable stress. You will see challenges and failures as an opportunity to grow and take pride in developing your professional skills.

This is what I call a "dream job" and I know that you can create this by following the steps set out in this book.

"It is impossible for *everybody* to have a dream job"

This argument is basically that we cannot *all* be fulfilled in our job. Job satisfaction is the privilege of a selected group of wealthy people or artists who have found their vocation. Most people have to work hard. In any event, if we all had our dream job, who would collect the litter and clean our toilets?

My answer to this argument is that we all have different needs and desires. What appears as a dire job to you may be a positive challenge or career step for somebody else at a certain point in their life. There are also many people who are not interested in career progression or the responsibilities that come with it. For some people, simplicity, predictability and security are enough.

In the end, though, this question is academic and irrelevant to *your* life. When I have a client in front of me, the only question I ask is how *he or she* can find a career they love. In that moment I do not care about others. I take it one person at a time. For you as the reader this means that the only question you need to ask yourself now is how *you* can improve *your* job satisfaction – if that's what you want.

Objections like those above are often used as an excuse for not even trying to find a more rewarding job. It's so much easier to say that it is not possible, because then you don't even have to try and you cannot fail. But how can you know that it's impossible to find a better job if you haven't tried? What have you done so far to create a dream job for yourself? How much do you really want it? Do you want it more than the comfort and perceived security you enjoy from maintaining your current situation?

Do not let your excuses keep you stuck in a job or career you don't enjoy. I invite you to work through this book and maybe hire a coach to help you create a fulfilling career.

Life is too short!

Chapter 3

Who this book is for

This book is for people who want to improve their job satisfaction. This can be relevant to all of us at various stages in our life. Have a look at the following employee stereotypes. Do you recognise yourself in one of them?

The Wage Slave

The only reason you work is to earn money. You are not engaged with your job and live for the weekends and holidays. You probably complain a lot and count the hours at work. Your job drains you of energy and you dread Monday mornings.

You may have put up with this for a long time and are now realising that you're wasting your life. You know that this simply cannot be all there is to life.

If this resonates with you, I suggest that you read the entire book from start to finish.

The Job Seeker

You have lost your job or are ready to change your current employment. You may not know yet what you really want or how you can avoid a repeat of the same problems you experienced in your previous job. You do not feel a strong passion that leads you in any particular direction, or maybe you lack a vision or a belief in the possibilities of an alternative career.

If you are at this level, you will benefit most from reading Chapters 7 and 8 to establish your values and life mission. Then move on to Part 4, which provides tools for exploring new career options.

The Victim

You believe that you are badly treated at work and you complain a lot. You feel like a powerless cog in a corporate machine that grinds you down. You may even be bullied or harassed.

If you are at this level, it's time to accept your responsibility for your job satisfaction. Understand your options and learn how to manage yourself and the situations in which you find yourself. For you, Part 3 about effective self-management will be most relevant.

The Ambitious

You have plans for your career. It's important to you that you are challenged and have opportunities to move up the career ladder. You are probably reading this book to find out how you can progress in your career.

The first checkpoint for you will be to establish whether your ambition is just about the status, recognition or money, or whether it stems from a genuine love for your profession. If it's the former, I suggest you start by determining your values in Chapter 7 and explore how you can boost your career by bringing it into full alignment with your values. Then create a personal mission statement in Chapter 8.

If your job is already a reflection of your true values and mission in life, you may wish to read Part 3 to improve your self-management and learn how to motivate your staff.

The Burnt Out

You feel drained from having given everything to your career for years. You have worked like a dog, long hours and weekends, neglecting the needs of your body and mind. Maybe you don't even enjoy what you are doing, but you see no alternative to staying in your current job.

If you have been living in this state for a long time, you may start to experience health issues, mood swings or depression. It's time to take action before you break down. Part 3 about effective self-management and Chapter 25 about your life balance will be important initially, but to really resolve your situation you will also need to think about your values and mission in life as suggested in Chapters 7 and 8. I also recommend that you seek medical advice if necessary.

The Entrepreneur in the Making

You want to leave your employment and start your own business; you just don't know what business or how to go about it. It's an exciting turning point in your life with wonderful opportunities, but also risks. Many business owners find that running their own business is not quite what they expected. They often work even longer hours with more worry – not just about money but also their responsibilities towards their employees. Running your own business can become just as much of a prison as employment.

My advice is to get the basics right first, and this starts with the "why" and the "what" of your own business. Go to Chapter 7 to establish your own personal values. They should be the foundation of your business. Then go to Chapter 8 to create an inspiring mission and to Chapter 19 to work out your desired life outcomes. Read also about self-management in Part 3.

The Leader or People Manager

You are looking for new ways to engage your staff. Maybe you are frustrated by work morale and believe that your staff are not reaching their full potential. Reading this book will help you understand what really motivates them (and it is not your company's vision and values!).

Part 2 will provide you with tools that you can use with your staff to help them understand what truly motivates them and how their work can fit into their overall life purpose. Part 3 may give you new insights into the various external and intrinsic factors for stress and motivation that determine how your staff feel about their job.

How to read and work with this book

If you have found yourself in any of the above categories, you can jump straight to the recommended chapters. However, I recommend reading the other chapters as well at a later point because they are all interlinked and you will benefit from them no matter where you are on your journey to job satisfaction.

Throughout this book you will find writing exercises that are essential to achieve the full benefit from the material. I mention effective self-management in various places in this book and it all starts with completing the exercises. It is your choice how deep you want to go and how serious you are about falling in love with your job.

You can download all the exercises in a single workbook from the website **www.LoveYourJobBook.com**. It means that you do not have to write your answers to the exercises into this book and you can print new copies if you want to revise your work. You will also find some other free bonus materials on this website.

This book contains a number of case studies to illustrate the points discussed. They relate to real people, but I have changed names, industries and sometimes the gender to protect their anonymity. An exception is Appendix 4, which shows a number of real-life examples of people who changed their career late in life. These examples were taken from sources in the public domain.

Chapter 4

My own journey to job satisfaction

The majority of my coaching clients come to me to work on their job satisfaction, and mostly they are looking for a new career that brings them fulfilment. I love coaching on this theme because I went through a major career transition myself, from being an employed lawyer in financial services to a self-employed life coach.

My life before that transition is a great example of how *not* to go about creating your career. I had to learn the hard way what it means to live according to the values of others and in ignorance of what was really important to me.

It took a major health crisis to shake me up and lead me to the information that you are now reading in this book. Once I gained clarity through the same exercises that you will find here, it became easy for me to break away from a career that no longer served me well.

The impact on my life was tremendous. It was like waking up after a long sleep. I gained a new sense of excitement and my days felt fresh and inspiring again. I started to live with purpose and a deep sense of fulfilment.

My search for a career

So let's go back to where it all started for me. When I had to decide on my further education after high school, I was like many people at that age. I did not really know what I wanted to do or what I was good at. My only benchmark was my grades at school. They ranged from average to good and none of them stood out. My hobbies were reading, writing, acting and listening to opera, but I didn't believe that I had any talents in those areas or that they could form the basis of a career.

I also had a strong interest in personal development. From the age of 13 I spent a lot of time exploring books about psychology, self-development and spirituality. From these books, I gained my first insights into human behaviour and taught myself meditation and yoga. I felt alone with this interest though. My friends had very different hobbies and my parents did not understand my passions either. I did not feel that I could talk to them about the things I read about and so it all happened quietly in my bedroom.

My parents did not have the awareness or skills to identify and support my interests and my school was not geared up to this either. I became indoctrinated with a view that I should go for a "proper" career like medicine, law or accounting. I learned that I had to be someone of a certain status to be of worth in society. My father divided the world into "masters" and "servants". Since he was a judge, he claimed for himself the title of "master" and he wanted me to become one as well.

Social pressure came also from my school. The parents of my schoolmates were all either academics or highly successful business owners. Most of them had significant wealth and I felt inferior when I was a guest in their villas in the posh parts of Hamburg. From those circles I perceived that being a business owner or executive was something even more respectable than being a lawyer or doctor.

Yet even as a child I was already doubtful whether I had it in me to rise to that level in society and become something as significant as a business owner, executive or, to stay with the concept of my father, a "master". I felt like an outsider.

My already low confidence suffered another hit through one strange event in my youth that I still remember vividly. When I was around 16 years old I shadowed a manager at a large tobacco company for one day as part of a school programme. I felt shy and uncomfortable all day. I don't think I asked many questions and was probably awkward to have around.

At the end of the day the manager called a colleague into his office for a reason I did not understand. That colleague looked at me intently, threw me a lot of personal questions and then asked for my sister's phone number. I can only imagine that this was some kind of test. Although I refused to hand over the number, it must have been obvious that I felt intimidated.

After the guy had left, my host told me that I was not cut out for being a manager. He said that the look in my eyes was too soft. I felt embarrassed and ashamed, and believed that he was probably right. At that early point in my life I decided that I was not made for the business world. I thought that I would be far better off choosing the "safe" path of becoming a lawyer like my father and my sister. I had no idea that in most cases being a lawyer means running a business and managing people too!

Living the values of others

I am sharing this detail with you because it is relevant to the subject of this book. What I went through is typical for the majority of young people, even though it may not always manifest in quite the same way. When we are young, we simply do not know what we want from life. We feel lost and overwhelmed by the choices ahead of us. What then happens is the following:

If we do not know what matters to us most in life, we adopt the values of others around us.

The above sentence is important for understanding the essence of this book. To illustrate what I mean, let's go back to my example. Because I did not know what kind of career I wanted to pursue, I decided on a career that was valued by people around me. My father and my sister were lawyers, as were many of my friends' parents, and I had the impression that society generally regarded being a lawyer as a reputable profession, with security, status and a good income.

We are bombarded with the values of other people all the time. We learn values from our parents, teachers, friends, our culture and religion. We also receive strong communications of values through media, such as advertisements, movies, magazines and pop songs. They show us what a desirable life "should" look like; what success means; what is beautiful; what we should buy; what we should experience; how we should love – the list is endless.

It's part of life and there is nothing wrong with being exposed to other people's values, but it is important that we **understand** that these are the values of *other* people and that they are neither right nor wrong. At some point in our life we need to take a step back and reflect on those values and decide whether they match our own.

When we live a life according to the values of others without truly sharing them, then we are setting ourselves up for a lot of suffering. I will cover values in more detail in Chapter 7.

My legal career

Coming back to my story, since there was nobody around to help me explore what I really wanted from life, I concluded that becoming a lawyer was a safe and worthy career to pursue, and that's what I did. There was a part of me that already doubted whether a legal career was right for me, but I felt reassured by other people's advice that a law degree would prepare me for a range of career options. I later learned that this was slightly misleading but again there was nobody around at the time to question the advice I'd received or to raise other options.

So I became a lawyer, which is a long process in Germany. You need two legal degrees, which together take around six years to complete if you are fast. Often you also have to wait for a year before you can progress to the second degree because it is linked to a training contract at one of the high courts in Germany and spaces are limited.

And that's not the end of it: Germans love degrees and to become a lawyer of excellent standing in the 90s, you were expected to have a PhD and ideally also an Anglo-Saxon Master of Law. I attained both. If you then added 18 months' conscription in the German military service (which applied to males only and has since been abandoned), a male lawyer was around 30 years old when he finally started working.

This is a long commitment if law is not your passion, but I did not know that. In fact I quite enjoyed the intellectual stimulation and the sense of achievement and pride I gained from my studies. I received a further boost when I landed my first job in a large international law firm in the City of London, in a legal system that was completely different from the one I was trained in. I fell in love with London and for a few years I was excited to live the "glamorous" lifestyle of a city lawyer working and playing hard in one of the most buzzing capitals on this planet.

Indeed, becoming a lawyer was not the worst thing that could have happened to me. In many ways, what I had heard proved to be right: it was a safe profession with a great income and status. There were many aspects of the profession I enjoyed and I was also good at it. Yet, after six years in private practice I became bored from the lack of growth and variety, and felt burnt out.

I had no ambition to become a partner because I resented networking, attending conferences and holding legal seminars. That's where it started to show that I was not really interested in the law or the practice of running a law firm. Like most city lawyers, I worked long hours, including weekends. I found it hard to make arrangements to meet friends because I never knew what time I could leave the office. The client was king and when someone called at 6pm asking for a contract that was needed for the next day, you would say "Yes, of course!" and stay as long as necessary, often into the early morning hours.

I played the city lawyer game for six years, but when the glamour had faded I was determined to look for other options. I saw my way out in becoming an in-house lawyer and with my credentials it was easy to find an attractive position. I became a commercial contracts lawyer for a bank in London. Again, I had a job with high status and great money. I was blessed with an amazing boss who believed in my potential and helped me grow professionally by providing me with healthy and inspiring stretches. After a year, she gave me my own team of contract lawyers to manage. I had finally become a manager despite my childhood prophecy that I was not cut out to be one.

The early warning signs

I am grateful for the experience I gained in both legal jobs. They were invaluable in teaching me a wide range of skills and business expertise, not to mention the dynamics of human behaviour in the workplace. Without this experience, I would not be able to support my clients in my coaching practice as effectively as I do now.

Yet, as much as I valued the experience in financial services, my work at the bank took a similar turn to my job in private practice. After the excitement of the challenge had abated, I was left with only the stress of a demanding high-pressure environment: a large amount of tedious red-tape processes, people ruling by fear, unreasonable demands, company politics and a lot of negativity around me. This was made worse by the fact that I did not really care for the products of the employer I worked for. Financial services never rocked my boat. The sole reason I took a job in this industry was because it was the only one that matched the salary I'd had in private practice.

After a few more years, the signs that something was wrong in my life became stronger. Can you imagine what happens when you give all your time and energy to a job you do not truly care about, being managed by fear and pressure from senior executives and surrounded by cynicism and complaints? Maybe you have experienced something similar. Many people have.

Typical early warning signs are lack of energy and irritability. Then often comes the numbing through alcohol, cigarettes, coffee, sugar, foods, TV, sex or recreational drugs. I did all of this! The situation is even worse if you do not have other areas in your life that maintain some balance. I did not have them. I was single and burnt the candle at both ends, going clubbing on weekends. There was a void in most areas of my life and I could not see it. I kept numbing it.

As you can probably imagine, this state is not sustainable for long. Your body does not let you abuse it and ignore your true desires for a long time. If you do not listen to the early warning signs, such as energy drops and mood swings, stronger indications will follow. In my case, they came in the shape of depression and attracting destructive affairs with unsuitable men. If you then don't listen to those signs either, you will eventually receive the hammer treatment that does not leave you with any choice but to change. In my case it came in the form of a disease called ulcerative colitis.

Two years of disease

Ulcerative colitis is an autoimmune and inflammatory bowel disease. I will spare you all the gruesome details but it is basically an inflammation of the colon which is regarded as incurable by western medicine. For most people with this disease, it takes years to receive a proper diagnosis, and this was the case with me.

Through years of growing symptoms, it did not dawn on me at all that they could be linked to my work and lifestyle. As my health condition deteriorated, I still performed my work duties, despite fever, pain and an inability to sit through a meeting without having to go to the toilet.

At the time when my symptoms became unbearable, I was part of a team that was working on a critical deal for our employer: the acquisition of a business part of another bank. We had been working on this deal for years and were close to completion. I thought that it was impossible to sign off sick at this stage in the transaction. I did not want to let my colleagues down. My team was understaffed and it would have been hard for any colleague to take over and catch up on the years of history behind this transaction, so I put the interests of my employer above my own health. In retrospect, it seems absurd that I put myself through this, but at the time I did not see an alternative.

In the end, my body collapsed. I was hospitalised and then spent 14 months housebound, battling with the disease. Quite ironically, the transaction I worked on, and that I had regarded as so important, fell through a few months after I took sick leave. The work of an army of employees who had been sacrificing their lives for this transaction for years through stress, late evenings and countless weekends was completely wasted; and somehow life at the bank continued even without the deal. What a surprise!

My case of ulcerative colitis was extremely severe. You know that you are in trouble when you have five medical consultants standing around your hospital bed, all excited about what an interesting case you are. I was flared up non-stop for about two years. The main inflammation marker used to measure the severity of the disease is the so-called calprotectin level in stool samples. A calprotectin count higher than 250 indicates inflammation. When I was sick mine was higher than 4,000.

The disease makes you shrivel away because your digestion is hindered. I lost 20kg, which was more than a quarter of my body weight at that time. For two years I would wake up every morning with nausea and thinking, "Oh no, another day of this. I don't know how to cope." I had problems eating and sometimes also drinking. At one point I checked myself into A&E because I could not take it any longer and asked for intravenous nutrition. I was at the point where I just wanted to die, but you don't die from the disease; you just continue to feel miserable.

Added to the physical pain was the isolation. I lost a relationship with a man I'd been dating at the time because I did not have the energy to engage with him in the way he wanted. I lived alone and had no family to support me in London. My life was limited to my flat, and my days dominated by my daily struggle to eat, researching treatments and watching endless box sets of TV shows.

At the worst point in my disease, the inflammation manifested itself in my feet. They became red, swollen and sore. I was unable to put any weight on them and for a few months I could only drag myself across the floor on my knees. Now I faced additional struggles. How to get into my bathtub to take a shower? This took me about 10 minutes each time. How to cook? I operated my stove reaching up from the floor.

Luckily, I could order everything I needed from the internet. It must have looked very strange for the delivery man when a man in pyjamas on his knees opened the door. Yet I did not even ask the delivery man to bring the groceries inside. I felt too shy and proud to ask for help. I just pushed each bag in front of me across the floor through my flat and into the kitchen.

In retrospect, I am amazed at how I coped like this for years, but for sure it dragged me down both physically and emotionally. I could not see an end to my situation. My doctor assured me that we would find a treatment that would work, but all the drugs we tried failed. We went through the entire hierarchy of drugs available for my condition at the time. I also invested about £10,000 in alternative treatments, such as Ayurvedic and traditional Chinese medicine, Emotional Freedom Technique (EFT), spiritual healing, Reiki and helminthic therapy. I tried various diets such as the Specific Carbohydrate Diet and spent a fortune on supplements and functional medicine testing. None of this seemed to work.

The turning point

After we had tried all the available drugs, my gastroenterologist had only one treatment left for me: the removal of my large intestine, which is called a colostomy. This procedure is regarded as a cure for ulcerative colitis, but it's a drastic one. The colon is removed, the anus stitched up and your stool excreted into a bag hanging from your belly.

The procedure sounded horrific at the time, but I was at a stage where I was close to not caring any more. I had read leaflets about the procedure and gradually made peace with the prognosis. There seemed to be plenty of people living fulfilled lives after their colostomies. I had not yet fully given in, though.

The turning point came at another low point in my disease. I was in hospital again and my inflammation was worse than ever. Once again, I was thinking that I would rather die when I received a Facebook message on my laptop. It came from somebody whom I had only exchanged messages with once a year before. I had commented on a book he had written about his own journey of overcoming inflammatory bowel disease.

His Facebook message contained a YouTube clip with Esther Hicks. She is a well-known teacher of the "Law of Attraction", a New Age notion that we attract into our lives that which we focus on. I knew her teachings well and they resonated with me, but I had not applied them for a long time. In this clip, Esther Hicks spoke about the connection between the mind and your physical wellbeing.

Something clicked inside me.

I had known about the ability of the mind to heal the body for quite some time. The placebo effect was sufficient proof to me that a body-mind connection existed. I had also received guidance from a meditation that my body would be perfectly fine healing itself if I just stopped making it ill. When I put all of this together, I realised that to defeat my disease I had to become serious about my mental state. I had to apply all the wisdom that I had accumulated over the last decades.

I came to the conclusion that there was a message in my medical condition and that I had no chance of beating it unless I changed my mental state. How could I become healthy if all I thought about was that I would rather die? I accepted that I did not really want to die; I wanted to live, and it was time to work on this. I also realised that I had to get out of hospital because everything around me communicated an aura of disease. The people on my ward were all severely ill, some much worse than I was, and one even died next to me.

After this realisation, I pulled myself together and started working on my mental state. I meditated several times a day, imagining white light entering my body and healing the walls of my intestines. I downloaded images of healthy intestines from the internet and visualised my own intestines returning to their natural healthy states as shown on those pictures. I visualised myself strong and healthy again, full of power and joy; running around my local park in the sun; dancing with friends; spending a romantic holiday with a lover. I gave my meditation as much detail and emotion as I could. The idea was to activate the healing powers of my subconscious mind by tricking it into believing that my visualisations were already reality.

After a few days practising the meditations, my medical test results improved. I was excited and encouraged to continue with my daily routine. My condition steadily improved and six months later I was in full remission and have remained so ever since.

I cannot say for sure that my mental exercises healed me as this is impossible to prove and I tried so many things at the same time. But I believe that they were at least a significant contributor to my recovery. In any event, that's not important for the purpose of this book. What happened next brings us back to the topic of job satisfaction.

Choosing a new career

When I gradually returned to normal life as a healthy person, the smallest detail seemed precious. I still vividly remember the pleasure of going to my local coffee shop again (on two crutches!) and sitting in the sun drinking a herbal tea. The next step was to venture as far as my local park and see the wonders of nature with a new intensity.

I was also excited to return to work. It was wonderful to finally live a normal life again. Yet I could not help but see my work environment in a different light now. I had become more aware of the negativity in my office. People working under pressure, in fear of their superiors, sometimes frightened to even take a lunch break; disengaged, cynical and all of this in crammed open-plan office spaces with no natural light. I could not help but ask myself: "Did I come back to life just for *this*?"

My answer was "no".

At that time I was working with a coach to rebuild my life. He was the best coach I could afford, at an eye-watering price for a one-year coaching package. It was the best investment that I have ever made. Coaching brings us clarity that is hard to find on our own because we are too close to our own issues. It helps us see how we function as an individual human being and empowers us to take charge of our life and create the life outcomes we desire.

My coach introduced me to the work of Dr John Demartini, an internationally renowned speaker, teacher and human behaviour specialist. Of all the personal development teachings and tools I have learned in my life, I find that his are amongst the most inspiring and effective.

When I had completed the Demartini Value Determination Process®, which is described in more detail in Chapter 7 and attached in Appendix 1, I realised what I had to do with my life. This process helps us understand what we value most by exploring where our energy and attention already flow naturally. It does so by looking at thirteen areas in our life where our true values are bound to show up.

By completing the exercise I established that my highest personal value in life was personal growth. I had been reading about this subject from the age of thirteen and since then had been spending a large amount of time and money on retreats and seminars at least once a year. I have always a felt a strong urge to work on myself and to help others to grow as well.

With this new insight, I looked at my life and realised that I'd created a situation in which I could not grow in the way I wanted. I felt trapped in the golden cage of corporate life, slave to an attractive pay cheque and not fulfilled by what I did. Other areas of my life were similar. In the years before my disease, I had spent most of my free time in clubs and bars, an environment in which I could not grow, and in relationships that held me back on my path.

I knew what I had to do. I decided that I wanted to take on a new career which was purely focused on the pursuance of my highest personal value – personal growth – and for me this was coaching.

I retrained as a transformational life coach and now help my clients to create similarly powerful transformations in their lives.

I love this new career. It's like a second springtime in my life. My days feel fresh and inspiring again. This does not mean that everything is always rosy now. I still experience stress, worries and challenges. Yet there is an underlying foundation of purpose, direction and satisfaction with my life that creates a wonderful sense of fulfilment.

It is this sense of fulfilment that this book is all about. If this appeals to you, you can create it for yourself too by following the steps I will set out.

It's a beautiful journey. Are you up for it?

Part 2

The big picture

In this part of the book:

- ✓ We take stock of your current job satisfaction

- ✓ We discuss the benefits of making your job an enjoyable part of your life

- ✓ You will explore what matters to you most in life

- ✓ You will create a personal mission statement for your life

Chapter 5

How much do you love your job?

Let's start by establishing how satisfied you are with your current job. The way you feel at work will be determined by a number of external and intrinsic factors which I will cover in more detail in Part 3. The combination of those factors will place your Motivation Levels somewhere between "vocational" and "angry"; and your Stress Levels somewhere between "energised" and "burnt out".

Where are you right now?

Let's see where you are on this spectrum. Go to the table below and mark where your Motivation Levels and Stress Levels are in relation to your work situation:

	Motivation Levels		Stress Levels	
Green	Vocational		Energised	
	Ambitious		Balanced	
Amber	Loyal		Bored	
	Bored/Cynical		Frustrated/Overworked	
Red	Resentful		Exhausted	
	Angry		Burnt out	

*(You can download this and all other exercises from this book in a single document on the website **www.LoveYourJobBook.com**.)*

Green Levels

If your levels are in the green sections of the above table, then congratulations! You are doing well and probably enjoy a high degree of job satisfaction. Reading this book will then help you become more conscious about the things that you're already doing well and give you the tools necessary to stay on this path as your personal and professional needs change. This book will also help you coach others to improve their job satisfaction.

Amber Levels

If your levels are in the amber section, it's time to think about what is not working for you. You are still in a good position because things are not so bad that you need to take immediate action. You can plan your next steps from the relatively safe place of your current job or business. Don't be complacent though! You are aware of the warning signs, and if you stay in amber for too long it will grind you down. Without action, sooner or later you will move down to the red levels.

Red Levels

If your levels are in red, you need to take action as soon as possible for the sake of your mental and physical wellbeing. You could be risking mood swings, depression or health issues. Your problems at work could also affect other areas of your life, such as your family life. Ask yourself how long this has been going on. What has triggered it? What is the situation telling you? Once you have come up with some answers, it's time to take action.

Case study: Re-engaging with your employer

Sally is a great example of someone who successfully managed to re-engage with her employer. She was working in a recruitment agency and firmly resolved on leaving. She had lost interest in her day-to-day activities, which involved managing 40 members of staff in her sales team. She also felt overwhelmed by the demands of her job. Sally decided to retrain as a transformational coach at the same school I attended. She loved the course and was eager to finish her diploma and set up her business so that she could escape her job as soon as possible.

Sally had a smart manager, though, who valued her contributions to the firm. She was eager to retain Sally. She understood that Sally was not in the right role, and needed a new stimulating challenge and more recognition. She offered Sally a new position in which she had no people to manage and could instead fully focus on the strategy for the business. She also significantly increased Sally's salary.

Initially, Sally was in two minds about this move because she wanted to focus on her new coaching career rather than on settling into a new role with her employer. To her surprise, though, she found herself truly enjoying her new role. She no longer had to perform the mundane job tasks that had been dragging her down. Instead she now works on strategic business development, which gives her the stimulation and fulfilment that she had been longing for. At the time of writing, her idea of setting up a coaching business has become less important to Sally. She feels fulfilled in her new role.

Unfortunately, not everybody has such a great manager who understands what is needed to re-engage their staff. If that's your situation, then be pro-active. Help your manager understand what you want. If you don't ask, you may never get it.

Chapter 6

Ditch your work-life balance!

You may be surprised that a book about job satisfaction includes a chapter with this title. Am I really suggesting that you abandon all hope of a work-life balance? The answer is yes and no. What I am inviting you to do is to remove the distinction between work and life.

Just figure this: With the exception of a small group of financially independent people on this planet, we all have to work. In fact, work is a dominant part of our life. If we assume that you are working 40 hours a week between the ages of 20 and 65, with three weeks' holiday a year, you will be working 88,200 hours in your lifetime. This equates to 10 years. Many people work even more hours than this, and the average retirement age in the United Kingdom is likely to increase to 70 over the coming years.

So if you are saying that work is just a means to living and not part of life, what are you doing in those 10 years when you are working? Are you really prepared to devote them to earning money in a job you do not enjoy? Do you want to postpone the "living" part of your existence to the few hours after work when you are often too tired to do anything other than collapse in front of the TV? Since you are reading this book, you probably want more out of your job than just money. Maybe you are looking for a wider purpose, a vocational career or just more fun and fulfilment while you're working.

Just imagine what it would be like if you enjoyed your job so much that it became a valuable part of your life. Sure, you would still need to balance it with other parts of your life, and we are going to cover this in Chapter 25; but it would no longer be a conflict between "life" and "work".

Have you ever met people who love their job so much that they are excited to get up in the morning and go to work? They are certainly not in the majority, but I know quite a few. Since I retrained as a life coach, I count myself as one of them. Would you like to be part of this group? How much more would you enjoy life if you had a job you truly loved?

Chapter 7

What matters to you in life?

If you want to find a job that fulfils you, then the most important question to ask is what matters to you most in life.

We gain *fulfilment* when we fill our life with those things that we value most.

It's that easy. Yet often we do not know what it is that matters to us most. In fact, most clients who come to me are looking for clarity about what they want from life.

How can a simple question like this be so difficult? My answer is that there are just too many voices around us telling us how to live our life. Our own true desires are drowned out by the sound of all those voices.

The voices around us

It starts with our parents and wider family. They promote certain lifestyles and values that they expect us to share. Like me, you may have been brought up with the view that only academic jobs are worth pursuing, or maybe your parents told you that you had to gain status in society by setting up your own business or creating a legacy. Maybe you were at the other end of the spectrum and your parents told you to "know your place" and play small. You may also have been told how you should live as a man or woman, what good parenting looks like, how you need to behave in society, and so on. The list is endless.

Many of us were then exposed to religious values that communicated standards about good and evil, right and wrong, sexual behaviour, the role of women, caste systems, martyrdom, and even how to dress or what to eat.

In addition, most of us will have been exposed to some sort of peer pressure. As children we were conscious of the things that were "cool" or "not cool". We feared standing out from the crowd for not doing what the other kids did.

There are similar pressures in adult life:

- Maybe you do not feel comfortable saying that you work as a waiter when you are with a group of bankers.
- Maybe you feel that you should be fitter or more spiritual like your friends.
- Maybe you are a stay-at-home mother who feels less worthy than her working friends? The kind of woman who believes that she should be able to be everything: the all-giving mother, successful businesswoman, and then of course the skinny and beautiful fitness fanatic.

Then there are cultural standards. As a post-war German child I grew up in a society that resented patriotism and instead cultivated guilt and humility, combined with a sense of negativity and romanticising of "Weltschmerz" (carrying a sense of the "Pain of the World"). This was quite different from the sense of national pride that I later encountered in the United Kingdom and the United States – not that I want to place one approach above the other.

Possibly the biggest influence in industrial nations is the media and entertainment industry. We watch films that show us fantasy stories about perfect families, rags-to-riches success and endless images of immaculate beauty and fitness. They also make us believe in the fairy tale of the one and only, the soulmate who will fix our life and stay with us forever. We get the feeling that we are missing out if we do not have the wealth, sex life, fun and beauty that is shown to us in magazines and advertising. The reality of life can seem bland and disappointing in comparison to the glamorous lifestyles that we admire in movies and on TV screens.

These are just some examples of all the voices that tell us how to live our lives. You can probably think of others that were, or still are, influences in your own life.

I do not want to demonise those voices. They are part of life and, when it comes to parenting, for example, they are important to our upbringing. However, it is essential for our wellbeing that we identify those voices and reflect on their messages:

- From amongst the many voices that influence you, have you consciously selected only those values and standards that are true for you?

- Do they create resourceful results for you?

- Do you feel inspired by these values and standards?

- Are you actually *living* them or are they just "shoulds" that drag you down by making you feel guilty or less worthy?

If your answer is yes to all the above questions, then by all means continue to live by the values and standards you have chosen. But if you answered no to any of them, it's time to reconsider those values and standards which may have been imposed on you by others, or which you may have outgrown. For example:

- You may come to the conclusion that the religious standards you grew up with no longer resonate with your own truth.

- Maybe it's time to look for new friends or even a new partner to remove yourself from a lifestyle that you do not enjoy.

- Maybe you want to stop voting for the political party that your parents favoured and find your own position.

- Maybe you are finally ready to accept that chasing an unrealistic body image does not serve you well.

Let's dive straight into our first exercise by taking stock of the values and standards that have influenced you so far in your life.

Exercise 1: The values of others

In the table below, write down the values and standards that have been communicated to you by each of the sources shown. Think about all the different stages of your life, from your childhood to the present day. Then write in the third column the feelings associated with each message. For example, your parents may have told you "Men don't cry" and this may have made you feel "wimpy", "unheard" or "unloved".

Complete the following table for each category:

(You can download this and all other exercises from this book in a single document on the website www.LoveYourJobBook.com.)

Source	Value/standard communicated	How did/does it make you feel?
Your parents/ family	*Example: "Men don't cry"*	*Example: Wimpy; unheard; unloved*
Your teachers		

Your school friends		
Your culture		
Your religion		
Books		
Songs/Musicals/ Opera		
TV/Movies		
Magazines / Newspapers		
Social media		
Your current friends		
Your work colleagues		

Your community		
Your political party		
Any other source not yet covered		

Now reflect on your entries in the above table. Do the values you identified resonate with you? Do they inspire you? Have they created positive outcomes in your life?

Strike through all the values and standards on your list that you either:

(a) no longer live by; or

(b) now want to drop.

This is your first step in establishing what is important to you and we will go much deeper than this later on in the book.

What is a value?

At the beginning of this chapter, I suggested that fulfilment means filling our lives with those things that we value most. From this it follows that once we know what our highest personal values are, we also know what to fill our life with in order to gain that much-desired sense of fulfilment.

So what are *your* values?

Before we establish your highest personal values, let me explain what I mean when referring to "values" in this book as I will be using this term in quite a different way from how it is normally used.

When I refer to values, I mean the things that we love most in life. For example, my top three values are personal growth, coaching and health. I know that when I fill my days with activities in those three areas, I feel inspired and fulfilled. Nobody needs to remind me to do those activities. I always find time for them, talk about them a lot and am eager to increase my skills in those areas.

I am conscious that this may be quite different from your understanding of what a value is. When people refer to values, they normally mean social or moral standards such as honesty, integrity and authenticity. This is indeed one way to define a value, but it's not very useful for the purpose of seeking fulfilment.

First of all, those generic social standards don't actually tell you what exactly you need to do to become fulfilled. For example, generic standards of honesty, integrity and authenticity won't help you find your vocation because you can express those standards in *any* career.

Even more importantly, you are in denial if you believe that you always choose honesty, integrity and authenticity over lying and pretending. Human behaviour specialist Dr John Demartini helped me understand that we embody each human trait and its opposite. For example, we are both honest and dishonest depending on the circumstances. Sometimes we act with integrity, sometimes without. Sometimes we are authentic, sometimes we are not. When we choose which side we are on in any given situation, we reveal what truly motivates us.

Let's look at a few examples: If you are a parent in the western world, it's likely you have told your child that there is a Father

Christmas. You chose to lie and you probably did it because, in that situation, you value tradition or the magic of Christmas. In other circumstances, you might have lied to someone because you thought the truth would cause unnecessary harm. Maybe the true value behind that choice was security or friendship.

Another good example is that of a job interview. Who is ever truly honest when faced with the dreaded interview question about one's most significant weakness or a failure? In that moment you express a high value for the job you are after or for the things that the job will provide for your life.

On the other hand, sometimes we may choose the truth even if it is uncomfortable. For example, you may decide to tell your spouse about an affair because you value your marriage and believe that honesty is required to maintain its quality.

Can you see now how our true values determine whether we want to be honest or dishonest in any moment?

Let's look at another social standard that is often referred to as a value: integrity. Demartini explains that we have integrity when we act in accordance with our values. It is the result of living in alignment with our values, not a value itself. So we still need to know what those values are that determine whether we act with integrity or not.

I hope the above examples clarify the point that social or moral standards do not really help us establish what matters most to us in life; it is those things that do matter to us most that Dr John Demartini calls values. As I mentioned previously, my own highest values are personal growth, coaching and health. A few other examples of top values that some of my clients have identified are family, finance, travelling, writing, learning, teaching, fitness, organisation, community, art and creativity.

Just for the purpose of this book, I am asking you to adopt Demartini's understanding of what values are. The application and benefits of his definition will become much clearer when we get to the Demartini Value Determination Process® in the next section of this chapter.

Establish your highest values

There are many processes available for value determination. Of all the ones I have seen, I regard the one by Dr John Demartini most effective. I use it so much and find it so helpful that I have acquired Demartini's official certification to facilitate this process. I am also grateful for his permission to include the methodology in this book.

If you want to find out more about Demartini's work on values, I highly recommend his book *The Values Factor,* which goes much deeper into the discussion of values and their application in all areas of our lives than I can here.

Most other value determination processes more or less require you to select values from a list of options and then to rank them in order of priority. I was always bewildered by this approach, since to be able to select your values from a list you already need to know what they are. In addition, most of the values on those lists are simply social standards that are not helpful in guiding us through life, for the reasons given in the previous section of this chapter. Last but not least, this kind of process is likely to make us pick the values that we "like" or think that we "should have". They are not necessarily the values that we truly live and breathe each and every day.

The Demartini Value Determination Process® works differently. It looks at thirteen areas in your life where your true value will already show up. Your values leave traces in your life and you will find them if you examine themes such as what you spend your time, money and energy on and what you always talk and think about.

If there is no evidence in your life of something that you claim to be one of your highest values, then you are probably not being honest with yourself. For example, you may know people who always talk about becoming a writer, but they never write. A person who has writing as one of her highest personal values would write. She would make time.

An example is an ex-colleague of mine. Although she was a lawyer working in the same demanding high-pressure environment as I, she found time to write fiction for children after work – without having any idea whether she would ever be able to make an income from her writing. Later, when she signed her first book deal, she cut down her legal hours and accepted a significant pay cut to create more time for writing. Today she has published seven successful children's books and I love seeing her radiating joy and excitement in pursuing her value of writing.

Case study: Stay-at-home mum

Joanna had been hoping to have a child for 10 years. When this deep desire was finally fulfilled, she left her career in accounting to fully devote her life to raising her son. At that time, motherhood was the most important thing in her life, much more important than her career. However, eight years later she felt unfulfilled. She compared her life with those of her friends who had created successful careers. She felt inferior to them and was too embarrassed to go to school reunions or show her resumé on LinkedIn. She now thought that she had failed in life because she gave up her career.

I explained to Joanna that she was giving herself a hard time by retrospectively assessing a decision made in the past according to her present values. She was blaming herself for having left her career when in fact that was the best possible decision she could have made because it was in full alignment with her values at the time. Since then her values have changed. That's natural, and a resourceful response would be to plan a new direction in her life rather than regretting her old decision to leave her job.

Joanna managed to make peace with this conflict. In fact, when she tried to get back into her career in accounting, she realised that it no longer matched her interests. Instead, she started working as a teacher and translator and enjoys this work in a way that she never enjoyed accountancy. She has created a new career that feels inspiring to her and fits into her life as a mother.

The lesson from this case study is that we must free ourselves from comparison with the lives of other people who have different values, preferences and life conditions. We may also need to reassess our own values as they change over time. We only find what is right for us by looking inside in the present moment, rather than outside to other people or to our past.

In the next exercise you will find out what *your* top three highest personal values are.

Exercise 2: The Demartini Value Determination Process®

Turn to Appendix 1 and complete the Demartini Value Determination Process®. Do not skip this part. This exercise is a fundamental part of this book and you will need to know your top three personal values to fully benefit from the rest of the book.

Testing your values

Have you completed Exercise 2? If not, stop now, go back and complete the Demartini Value Determination Process®.

If you have done the exercise and worked out your top three personal values, let's test your results as follows:

1. If I were to look at your life as an outsider, would I see evidence of your top three values in your life or are they just fantasies in your mind? If there are no external manifestations or signs that you are actually living by, or working towards, those values, then they may really be just a fantasy. Be honest with yourself. Where does your energy *really* flow as opposed to where you think it *"should"* flow?

2. Sometimes my clients come up with values that are too generic; for example, "love". For sure, love is probably the most important value to all of us, but for this exercise we need to be more specific. What or who exactly do you love? Is it your family, your partner, your community, your profession or an activity?

3. Some clients come up with values such as "excitement", "inspiration", "self-worth" or "fulfilment". If that's you, I also have to send you back to do the exercise again. These are all states that are the *result* of pursing your values. They are not values in themselves. So look at your answers to the questions in Appendix 1 again. Ask yourself what they tell you about what you need to do to feel excited, inspired, fulfilled and worthy.

How can your values help you?

Once you know what your top three personal values are, you also know what you need to do to gain a sense of fulfilment in life. You need to create a life that enables you to pursue and express those values as much as possible.

When I learned that personal growth was my highest personal value, I decided to choose a new career that allowed me to pursue this value every day. The things that I love doing most are now at the core of my profession: reading about personal development, working on my own personal development, receiving training in personal development and coaching others to develop personally. I could have explored ways to express this value in my old job in financial services, for sure, but my desire for personal development was so strong that I wanted to go for the "real thing" and become a life coach.

In the next chapter, we are going to use your values to create an exciting mission for your life. Your values also have other applications. They can guide you like a compass in all sorts of decisions; for example, when choosing a relationship, a place to live or a holiday destination. When faced with a decision, you can always ask yourself how each option would support you to express your top three personal values.

Understanding your values and those of the people you are in contact with will also help you improve your communication skills. You will become a much better influencer if you are able to articulate what you want (your values) with reference to the values of the person you want to influence.

These and other applications of the Demartini Value Determination Process® are outside the scope of this book, but you can read more about them in Demartini's book *The Values Factor*.

Case Study: Knowing your core values

Jack came to see me because he was looking for a career change. He had been running his own IT business for 15 years and no longer enjoyed it. In particular, he resented the sales aspects of his business and the frequent travels abroad. Business was declining and I wondered whether this was a result of Jack's emotional detachment from his work. I could see that his energetic vibration was low. His voice was flat, he avoided eye contact and displayed a closed body language when he spoke about his business. Jack shared a number of ideas for alternative careers, but none of them seemed to really fire him up.

When I took him through the Demartini Value Determination Process®, we established that his highest core value was finance. He was very knowledgeable about personal finance, loved reading about it all the time in books and magazines, and often advised his friends on financial matters. We then used the Dream Job Formula™ from Chapter 21 to explore what kind of job or business would allow him to express those core values professionally.

It was fascinating to see the shift in his energy after we completed the exercise. The next time I saw Jack, he had come up with a list of possible careers that related to finance and the words poured out of him in excitement. There was a new spark in his eyes and he was diligent and effective in taking the actions that we agreed upon in each session. Jack told me that the Demartini Value Determination Process® had helped him realise what he needed to do.

I asked whether it had just confirmed what he already knew, because his interest for finance showed up so clearly in the answers to the values questionnaire in Appendix 1, but Jack said he had not seen it before. If I had just asked him what he loved doing, he would have come up with activities in the area of fitness and nutrition. He had not seen how much he thrived when he was occupying himself with financial matters.

I cannot wait to see what Jack will now do with the passion he has found.

Chapter 8

Create your personal mission in life

In Chapter 6, I introduced you to the concept of making your work a valuable *part of your life* as opposed to just a *means* to living. If you want to get to the point where you see your work in that way, you need to establish what you really want from life.

You started this work by establishing your highest personal values in Chapter 7. Now it's time to become more specific and decide how you want to express them. Let's create a personal mission statement for your life.

What is a personal mission statement?

You may know mission statements from the corporate world, where they are used to communicate the purpose of the organisation to employees and the outside world. People like you and I can have a mission statement too and that's what I refer to as a *"personal* mission statement".

A personal mission statement is a description of how you want to live your life, both at work and outside work. It defines the overall purpose and meaning that you wish to give your life. Note that I am assuming that *we*, rather than an external spiritual power, determine our purpose in life. You may have a different belief and in this case your mission statement could reflect the mission that you believe is *given* to you. But be careful with this. As I mentioned in Chapter 7, you could find yourself applying the values of your religion or spiritual teacher to your life. Reflect on those values to establish whether you really love living them. If you adopt values that you think you "should" be living, you will live the values of others and this will drag you down over time.

Personally I believe that *we* determine the purpose of our lives. I love the empowerment and accountability that comes with this belief. Yes, things will happen to us that we cannot control, but we always have a choice how to respond, what to think and what meaning to give to our life.

Having a personal mission provides you with a framework and compass for your life. As with the values work from Chapter 7, it gives you a sense of identity and direction. It also enables you to see how your work fits into your overall purpose in life; and once you can clearly see this, you will have a completely different relationship to your career. It becomes meaningful. You are no longer just working to fulfil the mission of your employer or business; you are working to fulfil your own personal and chosen mission. Does this excite you as you read this?

As an example, I would like to share my own personal mission statement with you:

"I am the creator of my reality. I take full responsibility for my life.

I live to create an experience of fulfilment, exploration and prosperity, for myself and my clients.

I find fulfilment and joy in leading and inspiring others to grow and create authentic lives that are true to their core values.

I devote my life to continuous learning. I strive to better understand and love myself and the people around me."

There are many ways in which you can write a personal mission statement and yours will probably look quite different to mine. It's important that it's meaningful to *you* and excites *you*.

Let's start creating your own personal mission statement, step by step.

Exercise 3: Your personal mission statement:

Each of the following steps is essential for creating a meaningful mission statement and fully benefitting from this book.

Step 1: Start with the end in mind

Find a place where you can be undisturbed for at least 30 minutes. Take pen and paper or a laptop with you.

The best way to plan your life is to start at the end! I invite you to use your imagination and time travel to the future, when you are 100 years old. You are still healthy, happy and have a sharp mind. Can you see how that future version of you would look? What are you hearing as your future self? What are you feeling? Get a clear image, sound and sense of your future self.

You celebrate your special birthday by looking back at your life. You feel a deep sense of gratitude and fulfilment as you mentally revisit all your past experiences. There are no regrets. You have filled your life with all the things you wanted to experience: a life fully aligned to your highest personal values. You remember how you were struggling to find your mission in life when you were reading this book and how you then decided to do this exercise and write a letter to yourself from the future; a letter that tells your past self about all the wonderful things you created for your life.

Over to you now.

Write the letter from your 100-year-old future self to your present self. Fully step into the role play and write full sentences as you would in a real letter. Don't take shortcuts by just thinking about the content or using bullets or paraphrasing. I want you to become immersed in the detail, the feeling, the vision and the creative process.

Approach the exercise with a playful attitude. Put aside any critical voice inside you that tries to distract you or keep your fantasies small. When we tap into our creative and visionary abilities, it is important to silence the voices in our head that are so quick to come up with objections. They tell us that what we are dreaming about is not possible, that it will never happen, that we are fooling ourselves or that we do not deserve to be happy.

Those voices have a place later in the planning process, but for this exercise they restrict you from freely exploring what you really want in your life. Park those voices while you are doing this exercise.

So get started now and write this letter about all the wonderful things that you are going to create between now and when you are 100 years old. Be specific and use descriptive and emotional words. Feel the gratitude and fulfilment as you are writing the letter, as if all the things you write about had already happened. Give it one hundred per cent while doing this exercise. You may never do this work again, so now is your opportunity to explore your dreams and desires.

If you are not great at writing, use a Dictaphone or the voice recorder on your smartphone or computer. You can then later have it transcribed for very little cost by using an online service such as upwork.com or fiverr.com.

Step 2: What do you want to BE, DO and HAVE?

Now that you have written the letter from your future self, you have a good understanding of the things you would like to have or experience in your life.

In the next step you are going to become more specific by listing what you will BE, DO and HAVE in the future life that your 100-year-old self wrote to you about.

Write down the following:

BE	Who you want to BE in your life	For example: • I am a loving mother • I am a successful entrepreneur • I am an inspiring coach and mentor
DO	What you want to DO in your life	For example: • I travel the world • I spend quality time with my family • I manage a flourishing accountancy business • I study history • I exercise three days a week
HAVE	What you want to HAVE in your life:	For example: • I have an annual income of £100,000 • I have a family home in London and a holiday home in Spain • I have a dog • I have a wife and two kids • I have 20,000 satisfied customers

A few tips for writing your BE, DO and HAVE list:

• **Present tense.** Write all items in the present tense. This is important. A vision will be most powerful when we write it as if we had already achieved it. Our subconscious will then look for ways to create this reality.

- **Qualitative words.** Use qualitative words that trigger a positive emotion in you, e.g. a _loving_ relationship or an _inspiring_ mentor

- **Alignment to your values.** Make sure that your DOs, BEs and HAVEs are aligned to the core values that you established in Chapter 7.

- **No right or wrong.** There is no right or wrong to the items you choose. Some of you may write about material things you wish to manifest, others about social connections, achievements in your career, sport or arts profession, spiritual goals or something completely different. Your goals are entirely up to you. Neither do you have to have to create a mind-blowing legacy for the benefit of humanity! This is about filling your life with those things that matter to you personally.

Here is my own BE, DO and HAVE list as an example:

BE	**What I will BE:** • an inspiring coach • a motivating speaker and writer • a loving and supporting friend and partner • the creator of my own reality • a lifelong learner
DO	**What I will DO:** • take accountability for my life • continuously invest in my own personal development • devote my life to serving my clients

HAVE	What I will HAVE:
	• a group of loving friends who equally support and challenge me • a loving and equal partner who supports and challenges me • an ever-growing group of inspiring clients who love working on their personal development and creating fulfilling and exciting lives

Now complete your DO, BE and HAVE list here:

(You can download this and all other exercises from this book in a single document on the website www.LoveYourJobBook.com.)

BE	What I will BE:
DO	What I will DO:

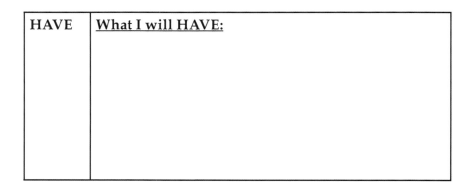

HAVE	What I will HAVE:

Step 3: Write your personal mission statement

Now we get to the main part of your personal mission statement. Sum up your top three core values, the vision in your letter from the future and your BEs, DOs and HAVEs in one overarching statement that describes how you want to live your life. We are only looking at a few succinct statements, not more than one or two paragraphs.

When writing your mission statement:

- write it in the first person, e.g. "*I* devote my life to..."
- write it in the present tense
- keep it short and simple

As with your BEs, DOs and HAVEs, don't let your inner critic restrain you and do not be shy about what you are writing down. You don't have to share it with anybody unless you want to. This can be your secret. It's just for you!

Your mission can be as small or big as you want. Not everybody has the desire to create a big impact on the world. Maybe your vision is just about your career, your community or your family. That's all fine; whatever gives you a sense of purpose and fulfilment. Don't put yourself under stress by thinking that you have to create a "legacy" for humankind!

Case study: Creating a legacy

Philip came to me with big plans. He wanted to break out of his job as an accountant and create "something big". His ambition was to create a legacy that brought people together and improved society. The problem was that he had no clue what this could be.

Over a few sessions we discussed various ideas, but none of them seemed to satisfy him. Either they were not big enough or they were too difficult to realise. It became apparent that his strong desire to leave a footprint in society actually prevented him from starting anything, because he had set the benchmark so high that it was difficult for him to settle on an idea.

We explored what was important about his dream and established that much of it was about his own ego rather than love for a particular project. I encouraged Philip to start with something small that he felt truly passionate about and then see how it could grow. It took Philip a while to become comfortable with the idea but eventually he agreed and set up a social group that meets regularly to discuss topics that are dear to Philip, such as social change, politics and philosophy.

Because this was a small and manageable first step, he was able to implement it with ease and alongside his existing job. It also still left him with time to explore other options.

Step 4: Test your excitement

If you have followed all the previous steps, you are nearly there. All that is left to do is to test your personal mission statement.

Is it exciting enough?

How much does your mission statement excite you on a scale of 0 (not exciting at all) to 10 (this is my dream life and I cannot wait to get started on creating it!). Be honest with yourself. If you rate it less than an 8, go back to the previous steps and ask yourself what is missing. What would make it a 10?

- Sometimes you will need to add another item. Maybe you missed an area in your life; for example, a loving and supporting relationship.

- Maybe your vision was not big enough; for example, you need to increase your desired annual income or include a statement about the social impact of your career to make it exciting.

- Sometimes it just requires changing an adjective to make an item more inspiring; for example, a "world-class public speaker" instead of a "successful public speaker".

If your excitement is not yet an 8 or higher, go back to all the above steps now, tell your inner critic to shut up, and extend, modify or refine your personal mission statement until your excitement levels are at 8 out of 10 or higher.

What to do with your personal mission statement

Congratulations!

You have created a personal mission statement. Now you know how you want to live your life and what is required to create a sense of fulfilment. You feel excited about your life. Maybe ideas are coming up already about what you want to do to bring your mission to life.

Here is how you can take this work further:

Where are you on your mission right now?

It is likely that you are not starting from scratch with the items on your mission statement. Acknowledge how much you have already achieved. How has your life been building up to this? How advanced are you already on your journey? Give yourself a pat on the back.

Then benchmark your current work situation with your mission statement. Can you see ways to pursue your mission in your current job and career? If your answer is yes, that's great! If not, what adjustments can you make to your career path to bring it into greater alignment with your mission?

You may come to the conclusion that you want to change your job or even your career to become better positioned to pursue your mission. Maybe your mission conflicts with your current work. In that case Part 4 will help you find a new job or career that is better suited to your chosen personal mission.

If you are not yet ready to change your job, be creative about what you can do in your current position. If your dream is to have a positive impact on your local community but you work in the head office of a bank, can you become involved in their community projects? Can you raise funds and inspire others to become active? Would you enjoy becoming involved in initiatives that will help the bank to treat its customers fairly?

You may also find that, now that you have a better idea of what you want, you will spot opportunities that you were not aware of before because your focus was somewhere else. It's like when you are considering buying a red car of a certain model and suddenly you see it everywhere on the streets. We are more likely to spot that which we focus on. Now that you are aware of your values and mission, you are likely to spot new opportunities too.

Keep it present and alive

This is the step where many people fail, but you won't be one of them. Most people who complete their personal mission statement lock it away in a drawer never to be looked at again, or it becomes forgotten somewhere on the hard drive of their computer. That's a wasted opportunity!

Keep your mission statement alive and present. Pin it up somewhere where you can see it every day. Maybe above your work desk, on your bedside table, on your fridge door, or make it your screensaver – whatever works best for you. The important thing is that you want to be reminded of your mission regularly.

I also recommend that you diarise regular reviews of your personal mission statement. Your values, desires and goals are likely to change through your lifetime and your mission therefore needs to be updated from time to time as well. A coach can help you stay on track with this.

Go to your diary and enter review point dates now; I suggest every six months. I have my review points as a repeating appointment with myself in my electronic calendar. My favourite date for reviewing my mission is 31 December. Each year on that day I reflect on my achievements during the past year, review my mission and values and set new goals for the coming year. I find that this is a great way to start the New Year with clarity, drive and inspiration. I know of others who love doing their review on their birthday.

Other ways of exploring your future

There are many different ways in which I work with my clients to find out what they really want from life. If a client has a strong creative side, asking him or her to paint or draw may work better than the letter exercise from this chapter. On a few occasions, I have given my clients a box of Lego® bricks to build a model of their future life. Choose whatever process and medium works best for you.

Sometimes I ask my clients what they would do if money was not an issue or if they had started their retirement. The latter question worked particularly well in the following case study:

Case study: Why wait until retirement?

Sylvia was a doctor and part-time partner in a medical surgery. She came to me to discuss various options for additional side incomes or new careers. She was full of ideas; for example, setting up a sexual health clinic, becoming a public speaker, writing articles and working on TV. I was then surprised when she told me in our second session that she was considering taking on a job as an in-house doctor at a law firm, where she was planning to work until she retired at the age of 55.

When prompted, Sylvia admitted that she did not feel passionate about the job she was offered but it seemed like a sensible choice to her. When I asked her what she was planning to do after her retirement, Sylvia answered that she would want to create a personal brand as an expert in treating sexual dysfunctions, including lecturing on this topic, writing a book and running a specialised clinic. This answer told me what truly mattered to her.

My next comment was about how she could do those things now rather than having to wait for her retirement. Sylvia hesitated and then the penny dropped. She realised that it would be a waste of time and energy if she postponed the things she really wanted in favour of a temporary job she did not care about. She had parked a lot of her business ideas simply because she did not believe that she could manifest them.

After that coaching session, Sylvia decided to decline the job offer from the law firm. In the following sessions we started exploring how she could bring her dreams to life.

At the time of writing Sylvia runs her own clinic treating sexual dysfunctions. She is writing a book on the subject and has had several appearances as a doctor on a TV reality show. She is also working on developing her own TV programme. Slightly more interesting than being an in-house doctor at a law firm!

Part 3

Falling in love with your current job

In this part of the book you will learn:

- ✓ about the benefits of positively engaging with your work

- ✓ what motivates you

- ✓ what causes you stress

- ✓ how to manage yourself more effectively

- ✓ how to motivate your colleagues

Chapter 9

Do you want to play or complain?

In this part of the book, I will provide guidance and tools for improving your satisfaction with your current job or career.

- Maybe you have decided that you can express your values (see Chapter 7) and pursue your personal mission (see Chapter 8) in your current position and you just want to work on the conditions and your own attitude and behaviours to improve your job satisfaction.

- Maybe you have a desire to change your job or career but not at this point in time, and in the interim you want to be able to manage your current work situation more effectively.

- Maybe you are already satisfied with your current job but you want to assist your employees to increase their job satisfaction.

This chapter will be useful for all of you.

If you do not enjoy your job, you have to make a decision:

Option 1: Do you want to leave?

Option 2: Do you want to suffer and complain?

Option 3: Do you want to make the best out of the situation?

If you want to pursue Option 1, then Part 4 of this book will guide you through a number of processes that will assist you in generating new career options.

If you decide against Option 1, then I strongly suggest that you go for Option 3. Option 2, suffering and complaining, is unresourceful and will lead you along a downward spiral towards resentment, frustration or even depression and burnout.

If you decide to stay in your current job or business, you can just as well play by the rules of the game and make the best of it. Just imagine you are at a party and everybody plays a game that you think is stupid. You can stand on the side and complain how pointless the game is and how boring the party. How much fun would that be?

Now imagine that you pull yourself together and join in the game. Could this be more entertaining? Would you feel a stronger connection to the other players? Would time pass more quickly? Maybe you could even find yourself enjoying the game.

When I worked in financial services, I did not really care about the products that my company sold. It was a retail bank and there is only so much excitement to be had about products that compete mainly through differences in interest rates. It was just money and figures to me, and this did not capture my passion or imagination. But I was firm in my resolve that for as long as I was in the game, I wanted to play it well; and I did. As a result I earned recognition and financial rewards, learned a wide range of skills and connected to extraordinary people. I could clearly see the benefits of engaging rather than complaining.

There are, of course, valid reasons for making complaints; for example, if you are subjected to bullying or if your working conditions are unsafe. What I am referring to here is the sort of whinging that only drags you down, as well as those around you, without actually helping to address or resolve a genuine issue.

Exercise 4: Engagement v disengagement

The following table will help you work through your feelings and understand your options when it comes to deciding whether to engage or disengage.

Take a moment to answer the following questions:

*(You can download this and all other exercises from this book in a single document on the website **www.LoveYourJobBook.com**.)*

What do you love about your job?	
What do you resent about your job?	
Do you want to engage or disengage with your job (delete as appropriate)? Be honest!	I want to engage/I want to disengage

If you want to engage, what will you do to improve your engagement? List all actions that could be useful in this respect.	
If you want to disengage, what will it cost you?	
If you want to disengage, what is your Plan B to improve your job satisfaction, e.g. changing your employer or career?	

If you have completed this exercise, you will either have a list of actions to engage with your current job or an idea for an alternative plan. The alternative plan could be to look for a new job or even an entirely different career. If that's what you are interested in, you will find exercises in Part 4 of this book that will help you exploring such alternatives.

In either case, you may want to get support to help you on your journey. Chapter 26 gives you tips about where to find such support.

Chapter 10

What determines how you feel at work?

If you have come this far in the book, I assume that you have decided to do something about improving your job satisfaction. That's great!

There are many criteria that influence how you feel at work and I group them under two headings:

- Motivation Levels; and
- Stress Levels.

Motivation Levels

Your **Motivation Levels** tell us how willing you are to engage with your work positively. They are influenced by many factors; for example, the following which could be termed **Motivation Factors**:

- How interested you are in the subject of your work
- How meaningful your work is to you
- How capable you feel in performing your work
- How well you are recognised and rewarded for your work
- How much you like your colleagues, customers and suppliers
- How much you can grow in your work
- How authentic you can be in your work

We are, of course, all different and there may be other criteria that are important to *your* Motivation Levels.

Stress Levels

Your **Stress Levels** tell you how much pressure you experience at work. As with the Motivation Levels, there are many factors that can contribute to this. These **Stress Factors** include:

- High workload
- Your ability to perform your work
- Time pressure
- Conflicts with colleagues, customers or suppliers
- Lack of sleep
- Lack of nutrition
- Lack of balance in your life
- Problems outside work
- Insecurity
- Perfectionism
- Lack of self-belief
- Problems setting boundaries
- Inadequate time management
- Fear of redundancy, disciplinary or dismissal

I am sure that some of the factors in the above lists are relevant to your work and there may also be others that are specific to you. The key to job satisfaction is to understand and manage those factors.

You may have noticed that some of the Motivation Factors and Stress Factors are generated by you, others by your environment. For example, your interest in your work and your insecurity are entirely within your control. They come from "within" and I therefore call them *"intrinsic factors"*.

On the other hand, the way you are rewarded and the workload you receive are factors that are generated from the outside. I call them *"external factors"*. We have less, or sometimes no, control over them.

Most people and organisations focus on the external factors for stress and motivation. Often people have an expectation that their employer should motivate them through rewards, recognition, promotion and opportunities. On the downside they then also believe that their employer is solely responsible for their stress levels; for example, through management of their workload.

Of course your employer has an important role in maintaining your job satisfaction, but there is only so much they can do without your cooperation.

Job satisfaction is co-created.

You need to take care of the intrinsic factors that I will discuss in Chapters 12 to 17. Your employer can help you with this, but ultimately it's *your* responsibility.

As far as external factors are concerned, you have limited influence over them. These are your options:

- **Option 1:** Move jobs
- **Option 2:** Influence your employer and colleagues to create change at your workplace; for example, by making suggestions, lobbying for change or inspiring others by acting as a role model
- **Option 3:** Increase your resilience to external influences

If you have decided on Option 1, then Part 4 of this book will assist you in finding a new job that you enjoy more.

What exactly you can do for Option 2 depends on your specific circumstances, and I am therefore not going to cover this in this book.

If you would like to work on Option 3, then Chapter 11 will provide you with tips on how to get yourself in the best shape for the dealing with external stress.

In Chapters 12 to 17, I will then discuss the factors that are under your control – the intrinsic factors for your Motivation Levels and Stress Levels. Taking care of them is the best thing that you can do for yourself and it will have a positive impact on your wellbeing and sense of fulfilment, far beyond your work life.

Case Study: Bullying at work

I appreciate that work situations can be complex and your actual options limited. My client Nina is a good example. She worked as an operational director for a biotech start-up. She loved what she did but was subjected to severe harassment and bullying by the business owner. This included public humiliations in front of the entire office.

Because of its small size, the business did not have a Human Resources department that Nina could turn to. All her friends advised her to leave the job, but she was adamant about staying as she was hoping to cash in on shares from a public offering of the company that was planned in two years' time. It was a hard choice to make and I recommended that Nina kept an eye on the balance between her wellbeing and the benefits of the potential pay-out.

Since Nina did not want to leave her job, we focused on survival tactics. Her work environment was clearly unsafe. Nina was also confused by the erratic behaviour of her boss, who on some occasions highly praised her performance

---

and on others attacked her aggressively. She found herself fighting for his affection and sometimes even blamed herself for his attacks. She had a breakthrough when I compared her behaviour to that of a wife who gets beaten up by her husband and still defends him.

The first step Nina took was to accept that she had done nothing wrong and that the behaviour of her boss was unacceptable. We then worked on strategies for establishing boundaries with her boss, which included standing up to the bullying and refraining from any banter on her side that could give her boss an opening for an attack.

Thanks to the survival kit that she created with me, Nina was managing to get through the days. Her situation was far from ideal, though. Nina realised that she would not be able to change her boss, but she still had choices: she could change her response to the bullying, take legal action or leave. But she did not need to be a victim.

A few months later, it became apparent that the pay-out from the public offering would only be a fraction of what she had expected. When she then also received an unfair appraisal, she decided to leave and managed to negotiate a compromise settlement. She later compared her situation to being at a blackjack table in Las Vegas: she kept losing money but wanted to stay at the table in case she got a lucky break. Sometimes it's time to stop whilst you have some chips left.

Just a month later, Nina found a new job that now provides her with a safe, healthy and stimulating environment.

Chapter 11

Dealing with external stress

Although you have limited ways of controlling external stress factors at work, there is a lot you can do to equip yourself to deal with them more effectively.

Are you in a peak state?

If you don't turn up at work in a peak state, you will find it much more difficult to deal with stress. Just imagine you arrive at work after an ugly argument with your spouse, or tired because you have not been able to sleep for a few nights. You feel under a lot of pressure and suddenly even a minor issue can make you snap or burst out in anger.

To get you in a peak state, you will need to take care of the following areas in your life:

- **Conflicts:** Any unresolved conflicts at work or in your private life will leave you with negative energy that affects your emotional stability. Wherever you can, make peace with the people around you. Not for their sake, for yours! It starts with proper listening and completely understanding and feeling the perspective of the other person. The quality of your communication skills will be critical in this respect. I will be saying more about this later in this chapter.

- **Lack of sleep:** Sleep is important for recovery. If you are deprived of the sleep your body needs, your energy levels and your ability to manage your emotions will be decreased. Make time for enough sleep and improve its quality through a regular bedtime routine. Avoid reading electronic screens before bedtime as they radiate light that will suppress your production of melatonin, a hormone which makes you tired at night.

- **Lack of water and nutrients:** Your body is under stress if you do not provide it with the amount of water and nutrients it requires for your physical and mental functions. Drinking lots of water and eating healthily is a beautiful way of loving yourself and ensuring that you are in top form.

- **Lack of exercise:** Exercising has many health benefits; it reduces stress and can make you feel better about yourself. It can also serve as a healthy way of releasing anger.

- **Energy suckers:** The main culprits here are caffeine, sugar, alcohol and recreational drugs. Caffeine and sugar give you an artificial energy high, but afterwards your energy levels will crash and you will feel even more tired than before. When you are tired, you probably need to rest. If you push up your energy levels artificially, you will create stress on your body systems.

  Alcohol and recreational drugs create a strain on your body in similar ways. They also adversely affect your performance while you are under their influence and often for some days afterwards.

  If you find it hard to get out of bed every morning, have look at your consumption of these items.

- **Depression:** If you are unfulfilled in your life, you may experience work as a drain on your energy and you may struggle in dealing with difficult situations. Make sure that you have something that is worth living for. This could be your career, a hobby, a personal mission or the people in your life. If you suffer from depression, seek professional help. It may just take a simple shift in your perception to gain a different outlook on life.

Improve your communication skills

Many conflicts at work come down to communications with your colleagues. The better your communication skills, the better you will be equipped to manage difficult situations that can otherwise easily stress you out.

This is a huge and fascinating topic. Here are a few cornerstones of effective communication:

Active listening. Communication starts with listening. I mean *active* listening. It's not active listening if you are just waiting for the other person to stop talking so that you can say what you have already decided on saying. Neither is it active listening if you are thinking about your next words while the other person is still speaking.

Here is a little trick that will greatly help you to hone your listening skills: Next time you want to practise listening, silently repeat in your mind each sentence that the other person says. While you are doing this, you probably won't be able to think about your next words at the same time. You will have to fully focus on theirs so that you can repeat them internally. It also means that you receive each sentence twice, once when it is spoken by the other person and once when you repeat it silently. This means that you are much more likely to take in the content and remember it.

Understanding the other person's position. When you listen, try to understand the position of the other person as best as you can. Go beyond their actual words. What are their real issues? What are they afraid of? What do they need from you? You may even want to repeat to them what you understood.

Once you truly understand what the other person is saying and what his or her underlying motivation is, you will be better equipped to support them, or to get your point across and achieve a compromise or settlement, if that's what you are after.

Acknowledge their concern. You can put the other person at ease by acknowledging their concern. It will also make it more likely that they will listen to what you have to say.

Speak to their values. Position your points in a way that speaks to the value system of the other person. Rather than explaining why your point is important to *you*, find a way to link it to something that is important to *them*. In a work context, for example, you may know about the key projects the other person is working on and about their performance targets. Can you spot an angle that will show them how what *you* want to achieve will benefit *their* goals? Can you create a win-win outcome?

Stay objective. It's worth examining how you talk to other people in various work situations, or even generally. For example, do you sometimes talk to people like a critical parent? This may well trigger a defensive or aggressive response from them, or they may simply refuse to talk to you. Aim for an objective and constructive communication style that focuses on issues or outcomes rather than expressed or implied judgments of the other person. This will make it easier for them to engage with you in a mature manner.

There is much more to learn about effective communication styles; if this is a skill you are interested in developing, I recommend reading specialist books about this subject or working with a coach to improve your communication skills. It will greatly increase your personal effectiveness and wellbeing.

Improve your time management

The better you manage to stay on top of the demands of your work, the better you will feel about it. Understand your priorities and design techniques of working in the most efficient way. I will cover this subject in Chapter 14.

Releasing emotions and pressure

No matter how well you manage yourself, there will be times when stress and conflicts get the better of you.

It is important that you find a way to deal with the stress and associated emotions. Here are a few ideas how to do this:

Exercise: As mentioned earlier in this chapter, exercising is a great way of releasing stress. Hit a punch ball or run for 20 minutes and see how much better you feel after it.

Journaling: Many people find it helpful to write about their emotions regularly. Once you capture your thoughts and feelings on paper, you may find that they no longer trouble you that much.

Talk to someone: This works in a similar way to journaling. Once you have shared the things that trouble you with someone else, you will probably experience a certain relief. This could be a family member, a friend or a professional like a therapist, counsellor or coach. However, be selective when choosing a friend or family member to talk to about these things. They may collude in the stories you tell yourself; for example, your complaints about your life and the people around you. They can also be judgmental and advise you from the viewpoint of *their* own values and agendas. A therapist, counsellor or coach is unbiased and will open you up to new perspectives on your life situation.

Meditation: A regular meditation practice will help you become generally calmer and better equipped to deal with stress and emotions. The more you meditate, the easier it will become for you to bring yourself into a calmer state. An experienced meditator will be able to calm herself down with a few breaths in any situation. There are many places where you can learn to meditate; for example, in mindfulness classes, Buddhist organisations or social groups on sites such as Meetup.com. There are also mobile apps that teach you meditation.

Walking: Going for a walk is great for calming you down as it will take you out of your stressful environment. You may want to choose a quiet place for your walk, such as a park. Take deep breaths, enjoy the nature and look upwards to the sky. Negative emotional states are associated with looking downwards, so if you look upwards you will immediately feel a bit better.

Breathing: Oxygen is even more important than water and food. We can only survive a few minutes without it. Yet when we are under stress we often start breathing flat. That's the opposite to what is needed in that situation. Take deep breaths when you feel stressed or emotional. You may even want to learn a few breathing exercises.

Have fun: Anything that you truly enjoy doing will help in alleviating stress. You could go dancing, watch a funny movie, meet friends, play a game – whatever works for you.

Stop the numbing!

Many people respond to stress by numbing themselves. There are many ways they do this; for example, by drinking alcohol, comfort eating, sex, gaming, watching TV, smoking or taking drugs.

While some of these activities can be completely harmless and enjoyable, be mindful when you are using them to escape and numb your emotional pain. It masks the underlying issue and prevents you from facing and addressing it. You cut yourself off from the warning signs that your body sends you. It is important that you listen to those signs, so that you can take action and avoid suffering depression, burnout or even disease.

Some of those numbing activities will also reduce your ability to deal with stress when you are at work; for example, alcohol and drugs, because they cause a hangover and a drop in energy levels. Consuming them regularly will make it even harder for you to deal with stress at work. They will pull you towards a downward spiral which can lead you to breaking point.

It's not easy to sit with your emotions, but numbing them just delays dealing with the underlying issue and is likely to increase the problem.

Chapter 12

How to motivate yourself

The most effective motivation comes from within you (**intrinsic motivation**). It is a drive to perform at work without the need for external motivation. Nobody needs to tell you what to do or to hold a carrot in front of you (although you should, of course, be fairly compensated for your services).

Intrinsic motivation is far more powerful than external motivation. You want to engage with your job because you love what you do.

You can improve your intrinsic motivation by working on the following areas:

Values & Mission

This is the most effective way to improve your intrinsic motivation. If you have done the exercises in Chapters 7 and 8, you have already done most of the work in this area.

Your motivation at work will skyrocket if you can truly see how your work supports your core values and personal mission in life. It can create a major shift: from seeing yourself as serving an employer to using the employment as a means of expressing your **own** values in the pursuit of your **own** mission. This is important, so I will repeat it again:

> *Rather than seeing yourself as serving the values and mission of your employer, I am inviting you to explore how your employment can assist you in serving your values and mission in life.*

So if you have not yet established your core values and created your personal mission statement, go to Chapters 7 and 8 now and complete the exercises you find there.

Seek inspiring challenges

Life is full of challenges. They are part of the human experience and essential for growth and learning. Just imagine a job without any challenges:

- Would you not be bored after a while doing the same routines over and over?

- Have you noticed that you are more productive if you are slightly outside your comfort zone, in a healthy stretch?

- Have you experienced how frustrated and detached from work you can become if you lack any sort of challenge?

I have for sure!

You have a choice whether you want to fill your life with inspiring or non-inspiring challenges. If you do not set inspiring challenges for your life, you are bound to find yourself faced with non-inspiring ones – and they will often be challenges created by other people's agendas.

Exercise 5: Creating inspiring challenges

Reflect on your current job. Do you have enough inspiring challenges that motivate you and help you to learn and grow? If not, write down below five challenges to seek at work over the next three months that will take you out of your comfort zone and increase your job satisfaction.

Next to each challenge write down what resources you need to complete them; for example, a budget from your manager, support from a colleague or any materials.

Finally, write down how you are going to reward yourself once you have completed the challenge.

	Description	Resources needed	My reward
Challenge 1:			
Challenge 2:			
Challenge 3:			
Challenge 4:			
Challenge 5:			

*(You can download this and all other worksheets as a single document on the website **www.LoveYourJobBook.com**.)*

Don't cheat by listing items that you are meant to do anyway or that are easy for you to achieve. We are looking for a *new* stretch.

Now start putting them into action! You may want to discuss your chosen challenges with your manager, who may be able to support you with them. You could also talk to friends or a coach about your challenges so that you have someone who will hold you accountable for actually completing them.

Build a personal brand

People who have a strong professional pride are much more likely to enjoy high levels of job satisfaction. I am referring to more than just being proud of your profession. It is about taking pride in displaying professional behaviour each and every day. I am suggesting this for your own benefit, not for the sake of your employer. It feels good!

On the other hand, do you know people who complain that they feel like a powerless tiny cog in the machinery of a large corporation? A slave who is exploited to create wealth for their employer? Do you sometimes feel this way? It's not a great feeling and another example of a mindset that can spiral you downwards towards resentment, frustration, depression and disease.

I would like to offer you a different way of perceiving your role in your employment. How about thinking of yourself as a one-man or one-woman business that serves a single customer: your employer? You take pride in your professional skills and the value you provide to the company stakeholders. You love improving your service and increasing your professional reputation.

A great way to achieve this is to think about yourself as a personal brand that you are looking to build and market. In fact, you already have a personal brand, because of the way you show up at work. I'm not talking about simply turning up to do your job, but the way you present yourself and the energy and motivation you demonstrate. This already communicates attributes of your skills and personality that people will associate with you. Hopefully, those attributes are already positive –but how about being a bit more strategic about this?

Have a think about the values you want to communicate through the way you show up at work. What expertise and behavioural skills do you want to be known for? How can you hone your skills to achieve excellence in your chosen area?

Once you have established the answers to these questions, create a strategy for consistently communicating or displaying those values, skills and behaviours at work, on social media and at professional networking events. They will become expressions of your personal brand. You could, for example, write professional articles, speak at public events, share relevant information on social media or just display those values through consistent action.

Exercise 6: Your personal branding strategy

If you feel inspired to work on your personal brand, you can get started by answering the following questions:

*(You can download this and all other exercises from this book in a single document on the website **www.LoveYourJobBook.com**.)*

What do you think are the values, skills and attributes (*positive* and *negative!*) that your professional environment *currently* associates with you? List at least 10 items. If in doubt, ask a few colleagues who you trust to provide honest and constructive feedback. If your company has a 360 degree feedback system, this would be a great starting point. You can also use one of the many 360 degree tools offered on the internet.

1. _____

2. _____

3. _____

4. _____

5. _____

6. _____

7. _____

8. _____

9. _____

10 _____

What are the values, skills and attributes that you *want* to be known for in your professional environment? List at least 10 items.

1. _____

2. _____

3. _____

4. _____

5. _____

6. _____

7. _____

8. _____

9. _____

10 _____

Identify the gaps between your answers to question 1 and question 2. These are your development areas for the purpose of this exercise.

_____

_____

_____

_____

_____

_____

_____

What *specific* actions are you committing to take now to close the gaps identified in your answer to question 3? Set target dates against each action.

Actions	Target date

Now that you have defined the skills, values and attributes that you want to be associated with, it's time to communicate your brand to the outside world:

- From now on make sure that all your acts, communications and outputs at work are aligned with the personal brand that you have created.

- Make sure that all your social media profiles and any professional website clearly communicate the values, skills and attributes that you decided on in your answers to question 2 in Exercise 6. If you do not yet have a profile on the professional networking site LinkedIn, set one up now. Make sure to complete the "personal statement" with a compelling and personal message written in the first person. You will find tips about using LinkedIn in Chapter 23.

- Consider writing articles, posting blogs, training colleagues, giving public speeches or even publishing a book that communicates your expertise and messages.

- Don't forget to take care of your appearance. Do your clothes and grooming support your personal brand?

Now that you have a strategy for your personal brand, how do you feel about it? Excited? Proud? I hope you do. It makes such a difference!

There are many books on personal branding available if you are interested in diving into this subject further.

Make sure you are valued

This item is slightly harder to implement. The degree of your job satisfaction will depend on the extent to which you feel valued at work.

Strictly speaking, validation from other people constitutes an *external* Motivation Factor, but I mention it here as part of one of the *intrinsic* factors as well because it is up to you to ensure that you are in a job or business where you are valued by your employers and customers. If you do not feel valued at work, have a frank discussion with your manager. Maybe he or she is just not good at showing you his or her appreciation, or maybe you just wrongly interpret the way you are perceived at work.

If you have established that your services are indeed not valued, then you may want to reflect on whether your performance is lacking. If, on the other hand, you are confident about your performance but unable to gain the recognition at work that you desire, it's time to move on. This is *your* part in the equation. The longer you stay in a position in which you are not valued or do not receive a fair remuneration for your services, the more you will resent your job and move along the downwards spiral of job dissatisfaction.

Have fun

Last not least, you will enjoy your work much more if you add some fun to it. Hopefully, you will already find fun in some of your work activities but let's add a bit of sparkle to it.

If you are one of those people who beaver away in front of their computer without looking up and talking to others, then give it a break. I actually used to be one of those people! Make an effort to chat to your colleagues. Get to learn more about their lives. Have lunch together and the occasional drink after work.

This does not come naturally to everybody, in particular if you're an introvert like me. In this case, make sure, if you can, that you have an extrovert in your team who loves to arrange socials, team exercises and brighten up the day with some light-hearted jokes and small talk.

This does not mean that your colleagues need to become your best friends, but I can guarantee that it will make a big difference to your job satisfaction if you make an effort to socialise at work.

Chapter 13

How you create your own stress

Stress is a key factor that influences how you feel about your work. We normally think of stress as something that is created by outside influences, but we also create a lot of stress ourselves through the way we think, the beliefs we hold and our behaviours.

Have you ever noticed that some people seem to be able to deal with stressful situations so much better than others? Ever wondered why this is? They may be in exactly the same situation as you but respond to it differently.

Some of this may be down to better organisation and other skills that they have developed to deal with challenging situations. If you think that this is an area you would like to improve, you will find ideas for better management of your priorities in Chapter 14.

I dare to suggest, though, that your internal mindset has a much bigger impact on the way you feel in a stressful situation than your organisation skills. Here are a few key topics that are relevant in this context and which I will cover in more detail in the next chapters of this book:

Motivation: If you love what you do, you are likely to be far more resistant to stress than somebody who resents his or her work. You are genuinely interested in what you do and appreciate the challenge instead of resisting it. Our internal resistance can add a lot of stress to an already demanding situation. If you do not yet know what motivates you, read Chapter 7 in which you will find out how to determine what matters most to you in life.

Perfectionism: If you set unrealistic standards for yourself, you can exhaust yourself pretty quickly. Nothing you do will ever be enough. How can it, as you strive for a perfect result in each and every situation? This not only generates a stressful expectation, but you probably also judge yourself harshly for simply not being "good" enough. It's a common pattern and we will look into this in more detail in Chapter 15.

Low self-esteem: If you have low self-esteem, you can easily become stressed about work because you already think that you will not be able to deal with the demands that are placed on you. You know you are doomed, that people don't value you and you probably resent yourself for being this way. I will cover this topic in more detail in Chapter 16.

Negative emotions: Any negative emotions that you are holding will add to the stress you experience. They may not even need to be work-related. You may feel frustrated or angry because of other areas in your life and bring those emotions to your workplace. Maybe you snap because you are still angry after a fight with your spouse or an incident of road rage. It is important to know that emotions don't just *happen* to you. You create them. This may be a new concept to you, but understanding this process and learning to manage it is key to living a fulfilled life. We will cover this topic in Chapter 17.

Some of these topics require a deep exploration of the way you function as an individual, but the good news is that the management of your internal stress factors is in your control. Understanding what they are and taking steps to get a grip on them will benefit you in many ways, whether at work or in other areas in your life.

Ready to have a look at each of them in the next few chapters? Let's go!

Chapter 14

Internal stress: Lack of prioritisation

Life is full of conflicting priorities and you need to decide where you want yours to be. If you are not clear about your own priorities, your life will quickly be determined by the priorities of others, e.g. your employer, customers, family or friends. This can be stressful and frustrating.

Clients often complain to me that they struggle to balance work priorities. They feel overwhelmed just by their normal day-to-day activities which leave them no time to do other things that are important to them, such as keeping up to date with industry news, attending training courses, developing their staff or thinking about their own career development. Sometimes they then work late into the night and over weekends to catch up with those activities, or they never get around to doing them.

Those clients then often ask me to help them manage their time better. While I do teach my clients tools to improve their efficiency at work, I also explain that this alone is not the solution to their problem. The nature of modern life is that whenever we create more efficiencies in our time management, the freed-up time is immediately taken over by other work. It never stops. We seem to be eternally busy.

I therefore encourage my clients to become clear about their priorities and make time for them. There are many ways in which this can be done if you are in a job that gives you some flexibility over the structure of your day. For example:

- **Set aside "me"-time**. You could remove yourself from your phone and email for a set hour every day, or at least once a week, to work on your professional development.

- **Do your stuff first**. Start your days by identifying the actions that will have the biggest impact either for you or your employer. If you can, prioritise those important items (ideally the ones with the biggest impact for **you**!). Do them first thing, otherwise your time can easily be overtaken by less important tasks or the agendas of other people.

- **Leave the office on time.** You could decide that on certain days every week you will be firm about leaving the office on time, no matter what happens, to pursue an activity that is important to you; for example, spending time with your kids, going to the theatre, working out at the gym or learning something new.

- **Be selective when accepting meeting invitations**. You could decline meeting invitations at work if your attendance is not strictly necessary.

These are just a few examples. Guess what normally happens when my clients claim this freedom for themselves? Nothing! The world does not go under, nobody complains and the usual day-to-day activities still get done. As a result of these simple changes, you can feel more in control of your day and more satisfied that you can pursue your own personal and professional agenda.

If you want to become better at managing priorities, the first step is to understand *your own* priorities. If you have not yet done so, go to Chapter 7 to establish your top three highest personal values and to Chapter 8 to create your personal mission statement. Then think about how your job can help you support your values and your personal mission.

Exercise 7: Your priorities

Complete the list below with your top five priorities for both at and outside work. Make sure that they are *your* priorities, not the priorities of your manager or other people around you (unless they truly match).

(You can download this and all other exercises from this book in a single document on the website www.LoveYourJobBook.com.)

Your top 5 priorities at work	Your top 5 priorities outside work
1.	1.
2.	2.
3.	3.
4.	4.

5.	5.

Now ask yourself the following questions:

1. How much is your life already aligned to those priorities?

_____

_____

_____

_____

_____

2. What do you want to change to make more time for your priorities?

_____

_____

_____

_____

_____

3. How can your priorities at work become better aligned to your own priorities?

_____

_____

_____

_____

_____

If there is a conflict between your own priorities in life and those of your job, you will need to decide where you want to set your boundaries. Obviously, there are limitations when you are an employee. Not every job gives you discretion about how to manage your time at work.

If that's the case for you, then have an open discussion with your manager if you feel that you can trust him or her. If this does not help either, then it's time to think about a different job or career that helps you take care of your own priorities in life better.

Chapter 15

Internal Stress: Perfectionism

Perfectionism is a fascinating internal stress factor. It is an issue so many of my clients battle with. I have to keep an eye on my own perfectionism as well.

A perfectionist always strives for a perfect result. This can be stressful because he sets an extremely high benchmark for himself. In fact, it is an unrealistic benchmark because nothing is ever "perfect". This leaves the perfectionist playing a game he cannot win. However much he may struggle, no result will be good enough.

This game is exhausting and it means that the perfectionist never really enjoys the fruits of his successes. He will always be critical of his achievements, thinking that he could have done better.

Can you see how this behaviour can create stress?

The game becomes even more exhausting if the perfectionist compares himself with other people whom he assumes to be high performers. There are three main variants to this game:

Comparing yourself with a person on a pedestal

You compare yourself with a real person whom you know and perceive as "perfect" or at least better than you. You see him or her shining from afar and put them on a pedestal above you. Maybe you admire a motivational speaker you saw on stage, that colleague of yours who just completed a high-profile deal with ease, or the power mother who became partner while coping with four young children.

However, often you don't really know those people. You adore them based on a small part of their life that you have seen. Maybe the motivational speaker is actually in debt and drinks in the evenings to overcome his depression. Maybe that colleague of yours made a number of significant mistakes when she closed the deal that will come to light in a few years' time. Maybe the power mother is resented by her children and abandoned by her husband because she neglected them for work.

We are all whole persons with positive and negative sides to our lives. Yet, when we are infatuated with the success of certain people, we often only see one side of them. We can create a whole fictional life story about a person based on just one happy Facebook picture. We then compare ourselves with the positive sides which those people show to the outside world. That's a fantasy; that person does not really exist. And a comparison with a fantasy is just cruel!

Even if that other person is indeed a better performer in all areas of their life, how does this matter to you? By all means take lessons from their success strategies, but without stressing out about having to be like them or even better. Honour your own path. Shine your own light. That's more loving to yourself.

Comparing yourself with a fictional person

Sometimes a perfectionist will compare herself with a person that does not even exist. Take a fictional hero from a novel, movie or TV show and compare yourself with her or him. That's truly masterful perfectionism.

Let's look at an example: Have you ever watched one of those US TV dramas that are about the lives of lawyers? The lawyers on those shows are always in top form (despite drinking every day!). They are knowledgeable in any area of law that is thrown at them and they can cite the most unusual cases from the top of their head. They are also shrewd businessmen, have athletic bodies, beautiful homes and exciting sex lives. In a nutshell, once again they are fantasies!

Yet so often we fall into the trap of comparing our lives with those fantasies. That's perfect fodder for a perfectionist. He will set the lives of those fictional characters as his new benchmark and do whatever he can to get closer to them. That's of course impossible, and we all know this. But at a subconscious level these fantasies can still create an unrealistic expectation of life.

Comparing yourself with everybody else

Another great way to beat yourself up is to compare yourself with everybody else on the planet. You decide that you will only be satisfied with yourself if you are better than everybody else. You feel that "good" or "average" is not enough. You are only worthy if you are the best.

That's not only a hard goal to measure and achieve, it's also a bit arrogant. What are you then saying about all the other people who in your opinion are "just" average or good?

Of course, if you indeed achieved your goal of becoming the best in a particular discipline, there is a good chance that your inner perfectionist will still not rest. He might still find a flaw to criticise you or set you the next ambitious goals that you "must" achieve to remain "worthy".

Whose voice is it, anyway?

Your inner perfectionist typically has an inner voice that drives you to do better. It criticises your performance, tells you to try harder and makes you feel guilty for not being perfect. It's worth exploring where this cruel voice comes from. Very often it comes from your childhood, for example from your parents or others who were involved in your upbringing.

There could be many reasons why you developed your inner perfectionist when you grew up; for example:

- Maybe you were told that you were lazy when you were little and you therefore adopted a high standard for everything you do so that you would please others.
- Maybe you were told that you would risk poverty if you did not work hard.
- Maybe you became a perfectionist because you wanted to gain the affection of your parents.

I recently covered this topic with a client of mine, and he immediately knew that the voice of his inner perfectionist came from his mother, who had criticised him for most of his life. Even though he is now in his forties and claims to have no interest in the views of his parents, at a subconscious level the messages of his mother still affect his everyday decisions and strong compulsion to overachieve. Do you already know where *your* perfectionist comes from?

It's time to face this voice and reclaim your life!

Exercise 8 at the end of this chapter will help you explore your very own perfectionist.

The attraction of being a perfectionist

For many people it is difficult to silence their inner perfectionist because he can actually create positive results. Perfectionism can be both a gift and curse. Perfectionists are often high achievers. The mental whipping they give themselves each and every day drives them to perform well. They then fear that their success in life might stop if they ever lowered their high expectations of themselves. Often they also fear that they might lose the love and respect of others.

In fact, there is a type of perfectionism which is called "adaptive", where the perfectionist manages to maintain a healthy self-esteem and productivity. "Maladaptive" perfectionists, on the other hand, react to it badly to the invoice voice that drives them to overachieve. They have low self-esteem and either drive themselves like a dog or, interestingly, procrastinate.

Procrastination means *to delay or postpone an action that we have to do or decided to do.* It often comes together with perfectionism. Because the perfectionist already knows that whatever he does will never match the standards that he has set for himself, the temptation is very high not to even try. Have you ever found yourself doing this? I certainly have!

No matter whether you are an adaptive or maladaptive perfectionist, it creates internal stress.

So how can you tackle your own perfectionism?

For some people, redefining what "perfect" means to them works. The next time you aim for a perfect result, define perfect as "an excellent outcome *within the restraints of the time and resources you have or want to spend on it*". Define a realistic benchmark of the standard you want and can achieve, and then celebrate if you have achieved it.

Read the following case study to understand how such a reframe can work in practice.

Case study: Redefining your standards

Emilio is a film set designer. His artistic standards are extremely high. He loves his work and wants to do his best designing beautiful and inspiring set designs. He is at an early stage in his career and works on productions with a small budget. This means that he has to be realistic about what he can achieve with the money available. In addition, he is given very short timeframes to produce his sets, as well as last-minute changes in instructions that sometimes require significant alterations to his designs.

As a perfectionist, Emilio finds it hard to compromise on the quality of his sets. He overspends on the budget and makes up the difference from his own money. He works long nights and weekends, far more than is justified by the salary that he is paid. He does not receive support from other members of the team and feels that he has to make up for this lack with his own resources.

This pattern has been going on for a long time and Emilio feels burnt out and dissatisfied with his work. He is even questioning whether he is in the right career. At the root of his problem is the attachment to a perfect set design that is impossible to achieve with the resources and within the timeframes he has been given.

When I worked with Emilio we created a new definition of what perfect means in the context of his work. We agreed that a truly perfect set design was one that:

- was of a high artistic quality *given the restraints* of time and resources;

- was within budget;

- was delivered on time; and

- did not exceed the hours of work that he was paid for.

By reframing what perfect meant to him, Emilio could direct the drive of his inner perfectionist in a positive way towards a more realistic outcome. In addition, Emilio worked on his confidence and communication skills to better equip him to stand up for his needs and make himself heard within the team.

A redefinition of your perfect standard is a useful first step in tackling perfectionism, but sometimes more work is required. You may have to go back to the origins of your inner perfectionist. The next exercise will help with this.

Exercise 8: Explore the voice of your perfectionist

Imagine that your perfectionist is a person inside your head that constantly pushes you towards unrealistically high standards.

- What does that person look like?
- How does it sound?
- How does it feel to live with its presence?
- Does it resemble anybody you know?

Take note if you have an idea whose voice it is. Maybe it's the voice of one of your parents or of a teacher at school.

Now write down what exactly this voice is telling you, for example:

- "You have to work hard"
- "You must be the best"
- "Average is not acceptable"
- "You are only worthy of love if you excel"

It's not necessary that people told you those things literally. They may have communicated these messages non-verbally; for example, through body language, the way they talked about the world generally or the context in which they gave or withheld affection from you.

(You can download this and all other exercises from this book in a single document on the website www.LoveYourJobBook.com.)

Write at least 10 messages from your inner perfectionist:

1. _____

2. _____

3. _____

4. _____

5. _____

6. _____

7. _____

8. _____

9. _____

10. _____

As cruel as your inner perfectionist may seem, driving you like a slave to reach for the unattainable perfect result, it will have a positive intention. Psychology tells us that our subconscious never does anything unless it perceives a benefit from it. This applies to all sorts of thoughts and behaviours, even if our conscious mind discards them as self-sabotage. Your subconscious always has a positive intention; it just does not always have the best strategy.

With this in mind, explore the positive intention of your inner perfectionist, for example:

- Does it want you to be loved?

- Does it want to protect you from poverty?

- Does it want to keep you safe from embarrassment?

Go deep inside to find your answers. Write them down below:

_____

_____

_____

_____

_____

Now that you have understood the positive intention that is the source of your inner perfectionist, it's time to understand that its strategy is not working. Write down below what price you are paying for your perfectionism; e.g. feeling bad about yourself, burning out, absence of fun in your life, and so on.

_____

_____

_____

_____

Finally, give power to a new voice inside your head that tells you a different story. Go back to the 10 messages of your perfectionist that you wrote down earlier. What messages would you like to replace them with? For example, if your perfectionist used to tell you "You must be the best", the new voice could tell you "I enjoy shining my own light" or "I enjoy taking small steps consistently".

Now write down 10 of those new messages that balance your perfectionist and reduce your stress levels:

1. _____

2. _____

3. _____

4. _____

5. _____

6. _____

7. _____

8. _____

9. _____

10. _____

From now on, whenever you catch the voice of your perfectionist giving you a hard time, I suggest that you disarm him with humour. Laugh about yourself, in a good-natured way without criticising yourself. Then make a mental switch to one of the positive turnarounds that you created above. This may take some effort to start with, but with practice you will cultivate a new way of thinking that becomes automatic. The following routines will greatly support the process:

- read your positive statements out loud every day, ideally while looking at your reflection in a mirror
- write them down every day
- meditate on them every day
- record them on your phone and listen to them as often as possible, for example while you are going to work, exercising or meditating

Just pick one or a couple of the above activities and perform them as part of a daily routine. The more you practise your new positive statements, the faster you will reprogramme your mind. Regular repetition is key as it creates new neural pathways in your brain. You basically rewire your brain to support the new way of thinking you have chosen.

It is also important that you make an effort to "feel" the statement as you say, read or hear it. Try to generate the positive emotion that you would feel if you already fully believed and experienced the truth of the statement. This will facilitate the programming of the new belief in your subconscious mind.

As I mentioned at the beginning of this section, managing your perfectionism involves deep work. If this is an important issue for you or you find that your inner perfectionist is particularly stubborn, I suggest working with a coach or therapist on this issue.

Chapter 16

Internal stress: Low self-esteem

This topic is similar to perfectionism in that low self-esteem also comes from a voice inside us that makes our life hard. In this case it tells us that we are not good enough, that people don't like us or that we are doomed to fail. There are endless variations on this.

Low self-esteem can affect your job satisfaction in many ways. Maybe you do not dare to speak up for yourself or to contribute your ideas in team meetings. Maybe you start to stutter or mumble when you have to report to a superior, or maybe you avoid resolving conflicts that drag you down. Low self-esteem can hold you back from showing up authentically and contributing the value you have to give. This is likely to affect your mood and can also adversely affect your career progression.

Even if you count yourself as confident, you will benefit from taking the time to work through the exercise in this chapter because we all have insecurities or doubts about ourselves from time to time. In some people, these feelings are stronger than in others and there are variations in our abilities to manage them.

The following exercise follows a similar approach to the one in Chapter 15 about perfectionism.

Exercise 9: Improve your self-esteem

(You can download this and all other exercises from this book in a single document on the website www.LoveYourJobBook.com.)

Write down 10 negative things that you sometimes think about yourself. These can include things that you know are not true when you rationalise them, yet they do pop up in your mind from time to time. For example:

- "I am not good enough"
- "I will never get that promotion"
- "I am too fat"
- "I am too thin"
- "People don't like me"
- "I am too old"
- "I am too young"

Do you get the idea? Over to you:

1. _____

2. _____

3. _____

4. _____

5. _____

6. _____

7. _____

8. _____

9. _____

10. _____

Now think about how those things affect you in your work. It could be that you are not confident to speak up for yourself, that you are holding back from contributing in meetings or that you get stressed because you worry a lot about whether your performance at work is good enough.

What is the impact of your top 10 negative thoughts on your work?

1. _____

2. _____

3. _____

4. _____

5. _____

6. _____

7. _____

8. _____

9. _____

10. _____

Now it's time to look at the upside. You know there are positive aspects of your personality and abilities. Write down 10 things that are positive about your skills, attitude and performance at work:

1. _____

2. _____

3. _____

4. _____

5. _____

6. _____

7. _____

8. _____

9. _____

10. _____

How does it feel to write down all those positive aspects of your personality and skills? Hopefully, it feels good. If you find yourself immediately discounting or doubting your list of positive traits, you may find Chapter 17 helpful; it provides additional tools for dealing with negative beliefs.

If you still find it hard to resolve your negative thoughts about yourself, you might benefit from deeper inquiry. It's outside the scope of this book to take this subject further, so I recommend working with a coach if you would like to improve your self-esteem.

The purpose of Exercise 9 was to create a more balanced self-perception. When you feel negative about yourself, you often just see your negative traits – and often they are not even true. That's an incomplete and non-loving perception of your abilities, aptitudes and personality. The more you honour your positive traits, the better you will feel. From now on, when you realise you're talking down to yourself, switch to a more balanced view. For example, when you notice yourself thinking that you are stupid, you can stop and think: "Well, I can't be *that* stupid since I passed my A-levels/my driving test/went to university/landed that job" or whatever.

If you indeed encounter an area where there is a need to address a skills gap, accept where you are right now in life, plan how to address the issue and take action. Then be proud of yourself for managing the situation like an adult and responding to it in a resourceful and self-loving way. I know this is often easier said than done, but it's a behaviour that can be cultivated. If you are serious about improving your mental wellbeing, you can change the way you treat yourself.

The better you feel about yourself and your abilities, the more you will enjoy your work. It also means that you will become more proactive and have the courage to contribute your ideas and stand your ground. This in turn will make you more valuable to your employer. As you experience the truth of this, your confidence and job satisfaction will increase. You will be on the upward spiral towards increased job satisfaction.

Chapter 17

Internal stress: Negative emotions

Your emotions determine how you feel at any given moment. Positive emotions like happiness, joy and gratitude support high levels of job satisfaction. Negative emotions such as fear, anger and resentment will adversely affect the way you feel about your job.

We are used to thinking of emotions as something outside our control, but this is only partly true. Whilst I believe that we can never fully control our emotions, there are ways to manage them and I will share some of them in this chapter.

Can you remember a day when you arrived at work in a negative emotional state?

- Maybe you had an argument with your spouse or got stuck in a traffic jam. You felt stressed or even angry and arrived grumpy at work, then continued to be snappy. Even the slightest problem like a printer jam could trigger an emotional outburst.

- Maybe you were perfectly fine when you arrived at your desk in the morning, but then became anxious when your boss called you into her office.

- Maybe you became angry when somebody dismissed an idea that you brought forward at a team meeting.

In those situations you may think that *somebody* or *something* made you angry and you just could not help your feelings. We are used to thinking of emotions in this way, but I would like to offer you a different perspective:

Your emotional states are always <u>your own</u> responsibility.

Nobody has the power to change your emotions. You generate them yourself.

Let's have a look at how this process works.

How we generate emotions

John Grinder and Richard Bandler, the creators of Neuro-Linguistic Programming (NLP), developed a great model that explains how we generate emotions. It is based on the fact that all outside events that we perceive through our senses are processed by us internally. As part of this process we create an internal representation of the outside event which can never be a complete representation of the event itself.

To start with, our senses have limitations. There is only a spectrum of information that we are able to perceive with our five senses. We then filter and analyse the information we receive, which creates an *internal representation* of the event, but not *a complete mirror* of it. Our emotions are then based on this incomplete internal representation.

Understanding this process is the key to managing our emotions. In NLP this is summarised through the statement:

"The map is not the territory".

It means that we use a map of the world that we have created internally. Since it is not an accurate reflection of the outside world, it can sometimes lead us astray.

The following diagram is based on the NLP model and illustrates how we process information and generate emotions:

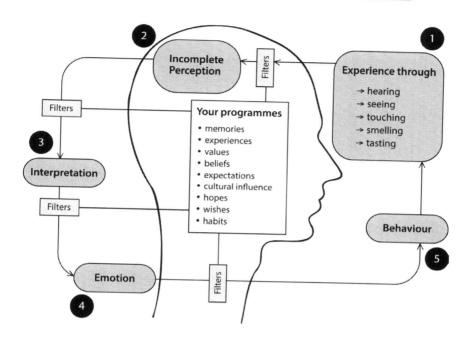

Diagram 1

It will be easier to understand this process if I explain it by using an example:

Let's assume that your boss is frowning while you are talking to him. It drives you nuts. You feel that he does not listen and believe that he has a low opinion of you. This makes you dread having your next conversation with him. You feel anxious and insecure. What exactly happens in your mind to generate these emotions?

1. **Your experience:** You take information through your five senses. You hear, see, touch, smell and taste your environment. The information you receive by these means

does not yet have any meaning attached to it. In our example, all you see is that the eyebrows of your boss move.

2. **Your perception:** You then filter the information you have received. It has been said that our unconscious mind is processing more than two million pieces of information at every moment, but we can only process about seven chunks of information at any time. This means that we have to filter the information to manage it. What we filter at any moment depends on a number of very individual factors, such as what is important to us, our beliefs, our past experiences and our cultural upbringing. Let's call these factors your "internal programmes". What they have in common is that they lead us to either delete, generalise or distort the information we receive.

In the example of your frowning boss, you may perceive that he *always* frowns like that and only when *you* speak, although this may not actually be true. Because you are so worried about your interactions with your boss, you discount all those occasions where he did not frown, or where he frowned when others spoke too. Your internal filters create a one-sided and therefore distorted perception of reality.

3. **Your interpretation:** Once you have filtered the information you received, you interpret it and once again you do so on the basis of your internal programmes. If you already have a programme running that tells you that you are not good enough and that your boss does not value you, then your interpretation of your boss' frowning will be an affirmation of those beliefs. You always knew he didn't like you and there you go, he's showing it again! Because you are so focused on this way of thinking, you are not seeing all the other possible interpretations. Maybe your boss has

problems concentrating, maybe it's just the way he looks or maybe he's having a bad day.

4. **Your emotion:** Your interpretation then triggers an emotion which again is determined by your internal programme. For example:

- If you feel superior to your boss, you may just think that his frowning is evidence that he is slow to understand and you may later joke about it to your colleagues.

- If, on the other hand, you have low self-esteem and already fear for your job, you may become anxious when you see him frowning.

- If you have a standard that tells you that the frowning by your boss is rude, you may become angry.

All very different reactions to the same situation.

5. **Your behaviour:** The last piece in the process is that you choose a behavioural response based on your emotion. This may be a conscious or unconscious choice. Let's assume that your interpretation of the situation has made you anxious. You started to sweat and mumble, made apologies and avoided eye contact. Your boss does not understand you and notices your lack of confidence. He makes a mental note that you are not up to the job. He brushes you off and you feel confirmed in your belief that your boss never liked you. Now that belief has become even stronger and will make you even more anxious when you speak to him next time.

Can you see how in the above example your internal process created the reality you feared?

There were numerous points in the process that could have generated a different outcome. Let's look at them:

- You could have concluded that the frowning was no reflection on your performance. You could then have asked whether there was a better time to speak to your boss or whether he wanted you to explain the matter again.

- Even if you thought it was personal, you could have decided that it was OK that he did not like you that much.

- You could have asked your boss what his frowning meant.

- You could have interpreted the frowning as useful feedback that you might have to improve your communication skills.

Can you see that there are many possible interpretations and responses and some of them are more resourceful than others? Which one you choose depends on those internal programmes or "filters" I mentioned; for example, the things you believe about yourself and the world around you.

Just to be clear: I am not claiming that you cause *everything* that happens to you. However, your internal processes have an *impact* on your reality. Let's look at another example to demonstrate this:

Imagine you are going into a job interview with low confidence. You think that you are not intelligent enough to land the job. You believe that your life is doomed and that the interviewer will find out that you are a "fraud". These are negative beliefs that will affect the way you present yourself at the interview. You can become nervous, lose your confidence and then maybe do one or more of the following:

- display closed body language
- avoid eye contact
- stutter or mumble
- sweat
- give incoherent answers
- send out negative vibes

At the end of the interview you know that you did not do well and so it is no surprise that a week later you receive a rejection letter from the company that interviewed you. At that point you see your negative beliefs confirmed. You always knew that you were not good enough and here you hold another piece of evidence in your hands.

Can you see how in this example your low self-esteem has led to a self-fulfilling prophecy?

How would the same scenario have played out if you had entered the interview with higher self-esteem? You might have done some of the following:

- been more assertive and chatty
- kept eye contact
- smiled
- demonstrated your genuine interest and passion
- asked questions that showed your engagement
- admitted development areas without feeling embarrassed

Can you see how in this scenario a different mindset could lead to different behaviours and possibly a different outcome of the interview?

Your beliefs

The examples in this chapter show how important it is to understand what you believe about yourself and the world around you. It will determine how you feel, how you behave and what you experience.

If you believe that you are not good enough, work is hard, people don't like you or your employer is heartless, than that's what you are bound to see in your life. Your subconscious mind is constantly looking for evidence of that which you already hold to be true. You are likely to discard or not even notice any evidence to the contrary and instead create new experiences that affirm your existing beliefs.

If, on the other hand, you have positive beliefs about yourself and the world around you, you will show up in life in a completely different way and your environment will respond to this accordingly.

From this it follows that, if you change your beliefs, you have a chance of changing your reality.

So how do you change your beliefs?

In Chapter 15 I already showed you how to replace the negative beliefs that may cause the pattern of a perfectionist. You can apply the same process for any other beliefs:

1. Establish what you currently believe.

2. Ask yourself what evidence you have that those beliefs are true.

3. Ask yourself what evidence you have that those beliefs are not true.

4. Write down how those beliefs impact your life.

5. Create a list of new, positive beliefs that you would like to adopt. They are normally reversals of your negative beliefs.

6. Cultivate those new beliefs through repetition, as described in Exercise 8.

Changing your beliefs can happen very quickly. It all starts with a strong resolve to change. In some cases, beliefs can be deeply engrained and be more difficult to resolve. A good coach or therapist can assist you with this process.

Exercise 10: Analyse your emotions and their triggers

(You can download this and all other exercises from this book in a single document on the website www.LoveYourJobBook.com.)

If you are struggling with an emotion at work, it is useful to understand your triggers and how you respond to them. This exercise provides a process for this.

Think of a situation at work where you were struggling with your emotions. For example, a situation in which you snapped or became angry, tearful or unpleasant. Let's have a look at this situation in more detail:

Step 1: Describe your trigger

Identify the trigger for your emotion. Be specific and identify the bare facts without interpretation. For example, rather than writing down: "My boss was grumpy", write down what happened to make you think that he was grumpy, for example: "My boss arrived in the morning without saying hello and slammed the door behind him."

Another example: Rather than writing down that your boss insulted you, write down what exactly he said; for example, that your work was sloppy.

Describe your trigger now here:

_____

_____

_____

_____

_____

Step 2: Describe your thoughts

Write down what exactly you thought when the trigger was pulled. For example, "I am not good enough", "I will be fired" or "My boss doesn't like me".

_____

_____

_____

_____

Step 3: Describe your feelings

Write down what you felt when you had the thoughts you described in Step 2. For example, "I felt scared", "I felt worthless" or "I felt angry".

_____

_____

_____

_____

Step 4: Describe your reaction

Write down how you reacted to the situation. For example, "I shouted", "I cried", "I lied" or "I apologised".

_____

_____

_____

_____

_____

Step 5: Describe the outcome

What was the outcome generated by your reaction? For example, "I lost my confidence", "I received a disciplinary warning" or "I was removed from the project".

_____

_____

_____

_____

_____

If you wish you had reacted differently in the above situation, then let's create a new strategy for you. Similar situations are likely to come up again. How could you react differently in the future?

New Strategy Generator

<u>Avoid the Trigger</u>

How can you avoid similar triggers in future? This will not always be within your control, but sometimes it may be. For example, choose different times to raise an issue with your manager; make sure that you are in a better mental state when you are at work.

<u>Think differently</u>

How can you think about this kind of situation differently in future? Is there a different way of understanding and interpreting the situation?

Behave differently

How can you behave differently in a similar situation in future?

Express your emotions safely

If your emotions still bubble up, how can you express them in a safe and constructive way?

If you find some of the above questions difficult to answer, I recommend working with a coach or therapist who can assist you with this.

The above New Strategy Generator will help you in two ways:

1. It will increase your awareness of how you function in difficult situations and this in itself may prompt you to think, feel or react differently.

2. Often we cannot come up with a resourceful reaction in a given situation. We are too tied up in the moment and later regret our actions. When we then think about the situation afterwards, we can see how we could have reacted differently. By analysing our behaviours in certain situations following the above process, we create ready-made strategies that are at hand when needed.

It's a journey

We will never be able to completely control our emotions – at least not at this stage of our evolution – but we can become better at managing them. There is nothing wrong with your emotions, but you will make your life easier if you learn to understand and then either transform or express them in a safe and constructive way.

Chapter 18

How to motivate your staff

You may wonder why I have included a chapter about staff motivation in a book that is about *your* job satisfaction. The answer is that motivated employees are not only great for business; they also positively affect the way *you* feel about your job.

Have you ever managed people who didn't really want to be at work? Maybe they were always complaining, counting the hours or had to be chased for their deliverables. What impact did they have on your mood and that of the rest of your team? One miserable member of staff can be enough to drag down the energy of everybody else around them, including their leader.

The good news is that there are plenty of things you can do about it. Rather than just taking a "carrot and stick" approach, consider the following:

It all starts with you!

The secret ingredient of staff motivation is *you*! You are one of the most important factors that influence the attitude and job satisfaction of your staff.

Here is how:

Your emotional state

If you have mood swings, feel stressed or tend to be grumpy, it will impact on the morale of your team. You don't even need to say anything; they will pick up on your energy. So take care of your own emotional state first. This may require you to look at what is going on for you at work and in your private life. A personal coach can help you with this.

Your own motivation

If you love your job, show your staff! If, on the other hand, you don't enjoy your work, it will be difficult to motivate them. In that case, it's time to ask yourself why you don't love your job and then do something about it. Work through the other chapters of this book to find out what you really want from life and your job.

Just imagine what a difference it would make to your staff if you radiated enthusiasm and passion for what you do at work!

Your behaviours

Act as a role model! People are known to copy their manager's language, energy and behaviours. For example, if you have a habit of moaning and making jokes about "those useless people in IT", your staff will take this behaviour as acceptable and quite probably start doing the same. Such behaviour can be infectious, especially when people try to bond by imitating you. What may have started as a light-hearted joke can quickly turn into a culture of moaning, cynicism and negativity.

Luckily, this also works the other way round. Sharing your enthusiasm and displaying positive and constructive behaviours can be equally infectious if done in an authentic way.

Treat your team members as individuals

When it comes to motivational strategies, one size doesn't fit all. There are different mentalities, learning styles, personal goals and values.

If a staff member thrives on social contact, don't leave her stuck behind a desk. Find job tasks where her social skills are a valuable asset; for example, networking or customer-facing roles. Another staff member may be a details person and become highly stressed when he has to rush or take actions without knowing the full picture. Use him for work that requires a thorough check of low-level detail.

You can explore the strengths and preferences of your team members through diagnostics tools such as Insight or Myers-Briggs, constructive one-to-ones or simply by chatting to your staff! My personal favourite is the Wealth Dynamics Profile Test of Roger James Hamilton, because it groups personality types into profiles that are easy to understand and remember. The test also identifies the other profile types that you need to have on your team to cover the aspects that are not aligned to your natural flow. I use it quite a bit in my practice and have therefore become a reseller of this test.

You can find out more and complete the test through my website: **http://hansschumann.com/wealth-dynamics**.   The test comes with a wealth of additional free online material. Contact me for group discounts at **info@hansschumann.com**.

Find out what they value

It's hard to motivate staff to commit to the values and mission of your company, because ultimately we are all only truly committed to *our own* values and mission.

If you want to engage your staff, I suggest that you find out what each member of your team values most in life. Then help them find ways to pursue those things in their roles. For example, if you have a member of staff who wants to lead teams, give her opportunity to learn these skills in her team. If a member of your team feels passionate about social justice, get them involved in your Corporate Social Responsibility Programme.

Show them how they matter

Most people have a desire to have an impact of some sort. Show them how they have that through what they do. Help them see how their contributions at work add value to your customers, colleagues and the communities your company deals with. Make it authentic and give specific examples rather than generic praise.

Promote a sense of professional pride

It feels good to take pride in your work. At your next team meeting try an exercise where team members can articulate what they are proud of in their work. Find professional values that are shared across your staff and use them to create a mission statement for your team that ties in with the mission statement of the company.

Staff can react cynically when mission statements are designed from the top. Mission statements are far more likely to inspire and be taken seriously if they are developed from the bottom and collaboratively involve all team members.

Reward and celebrate success

This does not need to be financial. Recognition and praise will go a long way. Show your staff how you value them and make sure to get the tone right. There is a fine line between encouraging and patronising praise.

Stay in contact

Have regular one-to-ones to stay in touch with what is going on with your staff, both at work and outside work. Learn about their challenges, successes and aspirations. You don't always need to make this a formal session. A catch-up over a cup of coffee can be equally effective if well managed.

Provide healthy stretches

Staff who remain in their comfort zone for too long can become bored and frustrated. On the other hand, if they are pushed too far beyond their comfort zone they can experience high levels of stress and eventually burn out.

Find a healthy middle ground that inspires them and provides variety and opportunity for growth.

Look out for warning signs

If you witness signs of frustration, resentment, irritability or high stress levels in your team, don't ignore them! Talk to the affected team members and find out how you can support them before negative sentiments spread to the rest of the team or health issues appear.

What if none of this works?

If none of the above measures work, it's time for a frank discussion with the disgruntled staff member about what he or she wants. You may even explore whether he or she would be happier working for another company. Be gentle though. Rather than confronting them directly, ask non-confrontational and open-ended questions that allow the relevant staff members to become aware of the issues for themselves.

No time for this?

If you think that you don't have time to implement the above ideas, then consider the costs of not taking action. How will it impact you, your team and your company if staff morale plummets? Can you afford to have team members who are bored, disengaged or cynical, or staff who become irritable, ill or make frequent mistakes because they are overworked? Can you afford to lose the staff you've invested in and begin the process of recruiting others?

What kind of manager do you want to be?

I have seen managers who are distant and rule through fear and pressure, and others who lead with their heart and vision. Which one is more likely to have a positive impact on morale and productivity? Which one do you want to be – and how will it make you feel?

Part 4

Finding a new job

In this part of the book:

- ✓ You will explore new career options using my Dream Job Formula™

- ✓ You will read tips about how to find your dream job

- ✓ I will discuss some of the objections and concerns you may have in relation to a career transition

- ✓ I will explore what a healthy life balance means to you

- ✓ We will look at some of the objections and concerns you may have

Chapter 19

Your life outcomes

In Part 3, you learned how to increase your satisfaction in your current job. Now we are going to explore how you can find a new job or career that fulfils you more than your current one.

Define your life outcomes

Before you think about specific jobs, I recommend that you start with the end in mind. What are the life outcomes you want to create? Many people almost stumble into their jobs and then accept whatever restraints on their life come with it. There is an alternative.

In the following exercise you can explore what you want your life to look like. You can then use these criteria to evaluate and eliminate potential career options.

Exercise 11: Your life outcomes

*(You can download this and all other exercises from this book in a single document on the website **www.LoveYourJobBook.com**.)*

Use the table to describe how you want to live. Rank the importance of each item on a scale of:

0 = not important at all

to

10 = I do not want to compromise on this under any circumstances

	Your preferences	Impor-tance (1 to 10)
General Lifestyle		
Where do you want to live? Think about the country, the town, location, and whether in a house, apartment or otherwise.		
How many days and hours a week do you want to work?		
What are your expectations on flexible working hours?		
How many holidays do you want to take per year?		
What hobbies do you want to have time for?		

What else do you want in your life?		
Who will be with you and how much time do you want to spend with them each week/month/year?		

Conditions at work

What kind of working environment do you like, e.g. home office, small suburban office, large city office?		
What kind of company do you like working for, e.g. large corporation, small business, family business, start-up?		
What job benefits are you looking for?		
What kind of career opportunities are you looking for, e.g. chances of progression, people management, training, exposure to certain types of work?		

What values should your employer have?		
How important is it that your employer has an ethical mission and is active in community work or other social responsibility programmes?		
How much commuting and travelling would you tolerate (or even like)?		
How many people do you want to manage, if any?		
What kind of people would you like to work with?		
What else is important to you about your working environment and conditions?		

Finance		
How much money do you want to earn?		
What assets do you want to own, for example a house, car, holiday home?		
Emotional		
How do you want to feel about yourself?		
How do you want to feel about your life?		
How do you want to feel about the people around you?		
Impact		
What impact do you want to have on your friends and family?		

What impact do you want to have on your customers?		
What impact do you want to have on your community?		
What impact do you want to have on society?		

Now that you have completed this exercise, you have a broad vision for your life and you can use it as a benchmark for your job hunt.

You may question the usefulness of this list. Maybe you think that the job market is not in your favour and that you are not in a position to make any demands. Maybe you think that you need to take whatever is available, no matter what the conditions are.

It is true that you may not be able to find a job that meets all your criteria. You may have to compromise on some of the points. The scoring you applied in this exercise will help you decide where you may be more willing to give. Yet you will also be surprised by what can happen when you become clear about what you want.

If you know what you want, you will be better placed to spot opportunities. Earlier in this book I mentioned the phenomenon that we tend to notice those things that our mind is focused on. A classic example is that once you consider purchasing a certain car model or new designer handbag, you suddenly see it everywhere.

It is called "selective recognition". The thing you are considering has become a focus of your attention.

Similarly, if you now know that you want to work in a certain city or for a certain type of company, your job hunt can become more focused and you may spot opportunities that you would have missed otherwise. Maybe you even feel brave enough to negotiate the terms of a job offer to fit your requirements.

Explore your options before you compromise. Don't leave it to chance.

Try *creating* rather than *finding* your dream job.

Chapter 20

Thinking outside your box

Most people are looking for a new employer who will hire them to do more or less the same they were doing in their previous job. It's certainly a natural choice but I am inviting you to also consider other options. If you are unhappy in your present job, staying in your current profession may just create more of the same.

How about learning new skills, applying for different roles or at least considering a different industry? The following diagram shows the range of options that are available to you.

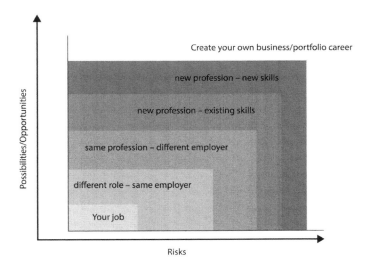

© Hans Schumann Coaching Limited. 2016

Diagram 2

The diagram starts with your current job in the bottom left-hand corner. From there, each larger box shows a wider range of job opportunities to the previous one, until you reach the endless opportunities of creating your own business or portfolio career. The wider you think, the more possibilities and opportunities will be available to you, yet the risks associated with your career change also increase. Those will mainly be financial risks and you will need to balance them against the disadvantages of staying in your current job. I will cover those risks in more detail in Chapter 24.

Which of the boxes in Diagram 2 are you currently thinking about? Would you be willing to consider other options? I am not saying that the options in one box are better than the others. For example, running your own business is definitely not right for everybody. I am simply inviting you to consider a wider range of possibilities than you may currently have in mind to increase your options.

If you are considering starting your own business, you may find the following case study interesting:

Case study: Starting your own business

The case of David shows that becoming self-employed is not always the solution. David was a partner at an accountancy firm. He was frustrated by firm politics, overworked and felt that his share of partnership income was unfairly calculated. When he was asked to pay £30,000 into the firm to improve the cash flow, he had enough and came to me to discuss an exit. His idea was to set up his own one-man accountancy firm. When I asked him what he was hoping to achieve from this move, he stated that he was looking for security, a better work-life balance and freedom from having to deal with office conflicts.

We explored how having his own firm would help him achieve those goals. When David reflected on the questions I asked him, he realised that he would actually have much less security being self-employed. Whilst he would no longer have to think about the financial risks of being a partner in a large accountancy firm, he would instead be in a position where he would never know where the next instruction would come from.

David also realised that his work-life balance might not necessarily be better when working on his own. Without the support of departments dealing with such things as IT, branding, PR and marketing, he would have to do all of this on his own and he knew that many small business owners find themselves working much longer hours than in their previous job. Finally, David accepted that he would still have to deal with personal conflicts. He would still need a secretary, suppliers and customers to deal with.

From this exercise, David gained a more balanced view of both the advantages and disadvantages of his current position compared with those of running his own practice. He decided to stay in his firm and instead focus on improving his relationships with his colleagues.

Chapter 21

The Dream Job Formula™

In Chapter 19 we looked at the life outcomes you want to create through your job. But you still may not know what kind of job you want to pursue. Many of my clients have a general dissatisfaction with their job but no alternative vision. They do not know what their "dream job" could be.

I have a simple process that will help you with just that. I call it the Dream Job Formula™. It works as follows:

1. List what you love doing (your "**Love List**")

2. List what you are good at (your "**Skills List**")

3. List companies or customers who want what you love doing and are good at (your "**Target Market List**"). These could be your potential employers or customers.

4. Establish where the three lists from the previous steps overlap (your "**Wish List**").

5. Write a list of jobs that match the items on your Wish List (your "**Dream Jobs List**"). These are your potential dream jobs.

6. Test your Dream Jobs List against your desired life outcomes.

We will go through this process step-by-step later in this chapter.

The following diagram illustrates how the Dream Job Formula™ works:

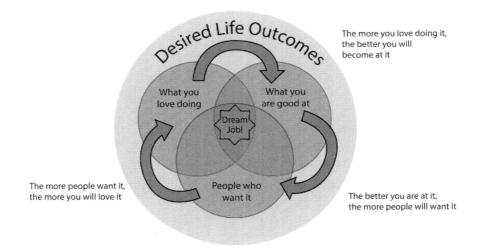

Diagram 3

The beauty of this formula is that it creates a positive upwards spiral: if you pursue a job that meets all of the above criteria, you are bound to be successful and feel fulfilled along the way. This is why:

- The more you love what you do, the better you will become at it.

- The better you become at it, the more people will want it.

- The more you see people wanting it, the more you will love it, which brings you back to the start of the cycle.

Let's get started!

Exercise 11: Finding your Dream Job

*(You can download this and all other exercises from this book in a single document on the website **www.LoveYourJobBook.com**.)*

Step 1: Create your Love List

List all the things that you truly love doing. They do not need to be work related. We are looking for activities that excite you. Nobody needs to remind you to do them. You are in a flow when you are focused on these activities and time flies by.

If you have done the values exercise in Chapter 7 you can use your top three values as well as your answers to the questions in Appendix 1 as a starting point. We want to go into much more detail here though. Identify very specific activities such as teaching maths, writing performance reports, advising people on social care, public speaking, researching environmental issues, cooking or travelling. Your hobbies should definitely be on this list.

Write at least 20 items:

1. _____

2. _____

3. _____

4. _____

5. _____

6. _____

7. _____

8. _____

9. _____

10. _____

11. _____

12. _____

13. _____

14. _____

15. _____

16. _____

17. _____

18. _____

19. _____

20. _____

Step 2: Create your Skills List

Now write down all the things that you are good at. There will be an overlap with your Love List as we tend to be good at the things that we love doing. If you are unsure where to start, have a look at Appendix 3 which gives you examples of transferable skills. Do not limit your choices to the items on that list though; they are only designed to give you an idea of possible skills that you might have. There are many more skills that human beings can develop.

If you are unsure what your skills are, ask a friend or colleague. Often we cannot see what we are good at because these things do not seem special to us. For example, my former colleagues often praised the structure and organisation I contributed to projects. This always puzzled me because I thought that what I was doing was just basic housekeeping. This is common: when we are good at something, it costs us so little effort that we cannot see how valuable it is to others. It is on the end of our nose but we can't see it.

As with the Love List, I want you to be specific. If you only think of yourself as, let's say, a doctor, lawyer, marketer, teacher and so on, it will become more difficult to establish transferable skills that have a demand outside your profession. Instead, break your skills down into specific activities such as "public speaking", "organising databases", "advising customers" or "project managing".

For example, you can break down the skills of a lawyer as follows:

- Advising
- Researching
- Creating documents
- Summarising complex issues
- Negotiating
- Structuring deals
- Understanding and managing risks
- Project management
- Resolving conflicts
- Giving presentations

All of the above skills are useful in many careers, not just the legal profession.

Let's look at another example. The skills of a waiter could be broken down as follows:

- Servicing customers
- Organising
- Crisis management
- Communicating
- Team working
- Teaching
- Taking payments
- Calculating money
- Resourceful problem solving
- Handling complaints

Admittedly, it may be more difficult to communicate the value of your transferable skills to a potential employer if you do not tick the standard search criteria for the new career you want to get into, but do not let this deter you.

Imagine you were an employer. Who would you rather hire: Someone with experience in the relevant profession or industry but who resents his job, or someone who does not have the experience yet but is fired up to learn and perform well because the opportunity you offer would enable him to pursue his passion?

Check out the list in Appendix 3 for more examples of transferable skills.

Now write down at least 20 skills you are good at:

1. _____

2. _____

3. _____

4. _____

5. _____

6. _____

7. _____

8. _____

9. _____

10. _____

11. _____

12. _____

13. _____

14. _____

15. _____

16. _____

17. _____

18. _____

19. _____

20. _____

Step 3: Create your Target Market List

Now have a think about the people or companies who need or want those things that you both love and are good at. I believe that for each skill we have, there is someone else who needs it. If you find people who need or want your key skills and are happy to pay the money you want to earn for your services, you have found your ideal *"Target Market"*. This could be either an employer or customers.

You may have to think outside the box a bit and this is where it becomes relevant whether you followed my advice in Step 2 to break down your general skills into specific transferable sub-skills.

Write down as many examples of your Target Market as you can think of here:

_____

_____

_____

_____

Step 4: Create your Dream Jobs List

Now look at your Love List, Skill List and Target Market List. Where do they overlap? What jobs would allow you to do what you:

1. love doing; AND

2. are good at;

3. for people who want it and are happy to pay handsomely for it?

This could be either running a business or being in employment.

Write down at least 10 jobs or professions that meet these criteria:

1. _____

2. _____

3. _____

4. _____

5. _____

6. _____

7. _____

8. _____

9. _____

10. _____

Step 5: Check your Dream Jobs List against your life outcomes

Now check the list of your job options against the life outcomes that you decided on in exercise 11 in Chapter 19. How does each option measure up against those criteria? Can you rank them? Do you want to remove any of them? Does this step generate new ideas?

Refine and restate your ranked list of career options here:

_____

_____

If you have completed all five steps of this exercise, you will now have a list of potential dream jobs.

If you do not have enough overlap between the lists you created, consider the following options:

(a) Be creative and think outside the box. Do the exercise with a trusted friend, family member or coach. It's often easier for an outsider to spot your talents and opportunities.

(b) Can you widen your "Love List"? Are there activities that maybe are not at the top of your list but would still be enjoyable?

(c) Are you willing to seek out further training, experience or qualifications to increase your skills and options?

(d) Are you willing to compromise on your life outcomes?

Some people find it easy to spot new career options using the Dream Job Formula™. Others require more time. If that's you, let the process sink in for a few weeks and then revisit your lists with a fresh mind.

It took me a long time to find my dream job, partly because I did not even dare to dream about an alternative life. I could not see beyond the boundaries of my current profession. If you have done all the exercises in this book, you have started a process that places you in a much better position to find your dream job than I was in when I started this journey.

Chapter 22

How to find your flow

People who have worked with me know that I often talk about the benefits of being in "flow". The term "flow" refers to our most resourceful state, when we achieve the most with the least amount of energy. We do what we love doing and in a way that plays to our natural strengths. Being in flow makes life easy. It feels light, inspiring and fulfilling. On the other hand, if we perform tasks that run against our natural flow, life becomes a struggle and we are much more likely to suffer burn-out, depression or disease.

There are two main parts to being in "flow":

WHAT you need to do to get in flow

This requires you to do what you love doing. We covered this in Chapter 7 where we examined what your energy already flows towards naturally. By pursuing those things we value most, we enter our state of flow. Nobody needs to remind us to do the activities that are high on our values list; we have no trouble getting things done and are likely to be performing well in those areas.

HOW you need to do "your thing" to be in flow

Once you know *what* you need to do to get in flow, you also need to think about the *how*. For example, I love coaching, but there are lots of very different ways to work as a coach. I could try to become a star coach like Anthony Robbins, who is often referred to as the father of the life coaching industry, and model all the steps he took to become successful. However, the same strategy would not work for me. I thrive better working in different ways than Anthony

Robbins, who shines when running massive, high-energy events with thousands of attendees. Although I can give a decent public speech and even enjoy it, in the long term it would drain me of energy. My core strengths are best utilised by doing deep one-to-one work with my private clients.

You have your very own individual personality that determines in which functions you thrive best. It's good to understand this. Have you ever wondered why others find certain activities so much easier than you? When you do the same thing, it costs you so much more energy and does not create the same results. When we have this experience we tend to judge ourselves, but it could simply be that the activity in question is not in our flow.

Some people thrive working in a front role or in a team, while others work best alone and in the background. Some prefer looking at data and processes, others connecting to people. Some of us are good at generating ideas, others better at implementing. These are just a few distinctions and it is useful to know what your preferences are. The same person who does that thing you admire so much with ease will probably struggle to do some of the things that are easy for you.

If you do not yet know what your most productive way of working is, you can find out by completing a psychometric test, such as Insights or Myers & Briggs. I use the Wealth Dynamics Profile Test by Roger Hamilton which you can access on **http://hansschumann. com/wealth-dynamics**. Contact me on **info@hansschumann.com** for group discounts.

The Wealth Dynamics Profile Test provides you with a comprehensive report and bonus material that will identify your individual personality and give you a clear direction on what path to follow in your job, business and investments. I prefer it to other psychometric tests because I find its profile types are easier to identify with and remember.

Once you know your most effective ways of working, you also know who you need to have on your team. It's most effective to delegate those tasks that are not close to your natural flow to those who feel in their natural element performing them. A psychometric test will help you establish who you need to have on your team to make up for the activities that are not in your flow.

If you work for a company, you could ask your manager or your human resources department whether they can facilitate psychometric testing for your team.

But isn't hard better?

Hand on heart: are you one of those people who think that things are only worth doing if they are difficult? If it's too easy, it can't possibly work! Does being in flow and trying to do it the easy way sound too lazy to you?

I must admit that I sometimes catch myself having such thoughts in some areas of my life. It's worth watching out for this, because if that's what we really believe then that's what life will bring us. Our beliefs determine how we experience life (see Chapter 17). We may miss easy opportunities, because unconsciously we always look for the hard way; then we are surprised if, after a few years of rolling our stones uphill, we feel burnt out and frustrated.

Life can be easy if you want it to be. What's it going to be for you?

Chapter 23

How to get that job

Once you know which job or career would provide you a sense of fulfilment and excitement, the next step will be to create a strategy for finding your desired job or starting your new career path.

Much of this will depend on your particular circumstances, like your personality, qualifications, experiences, network and the profession and industry that you are interested in. For this reason I am not able to give you a one-size-fits-all strategy for landing the dream job you are set on finding. I have a few ideas, though, that will get you started:

Recruitment agencies

Talk to recruitment agencies that specialise in the profession or industry you are interested in. They can tell you what qualifications or experiences are expected and may even have a job for you. Take their advice with a pinch of salt, though. Many recruitment agents may discard you as an unsuitable candidate if you do not tick their rigid search criteria. If you are thinking about a career change, it is quite likely that you will not yet have the qualifications and experience they are looking for.

This does not need to be the end of your dream, though. It could just require a mixture of creative thinking, approaching employers directly with a convincing pitch, leveraging your connections, having confidence and a bit of luck.

Your own network

Talk to people you already know in the profession or industry. They can give you a good idea of what it is really like to work in the job you aspire to. Like recruiters, they can also tell you about specific skills or qualifications you need. Maybe they even know about suitable vacancies in the company they work for or are happy to support you with a reference or introduction.

I mentioned earlier in this chapter that you may need a bit of luck when looking for a job in a different career for which you do not yet have the necessary qualifications. Your chances will increase with each person to whom you speak about your ambition, because that person may have some useful advice, be able to help you or know someone else who can.

In Chapter 26, you will find an exercise about identifying people who you already know and who can help you on your journey to finding excitement and fulfilment in your career.

Networking in the industry

You could start mingling with people in the industry you want to move into. Where do people in your desired profession or industry hang out? This could be, for example, trade fairs, conferences, speaking events, clubs or social events that are advertised on websites such as Meetup.com. If you need an invitation to attend an event you are interested in, find someone who can get you one.

Admittedly, this course of action is time-intensive and it will work better if you are extroverted and a natural networker. You will need to be confident enough to approach strangers and talk to them about your ambitions.

Internet

The internet gives you plenty of ways to research your desired profession and industry. You can resource market players and qualification requirements, find announcements of job vacancies and join relevant discussion groups.

LinkedIn

This is my favourite resource. LinkedIn.com is a professional networking site, a bit like Facebook but for work purposes only. Professionals can set up personal profiles that show their experiences and describe what they are looking for. They can connect to other professionals, share knowledge, publish articles and look for new career opportunities.

Most recruitment agencies search LinkedIn to look for job candidates and apparently many vacancies are not even advertised anywhere else any more. For this reason, I strongly recommend that you create a compelling LinkedIn profile. If you are looking for guidance on how to go about this, I recommend the book *How to Build the Ultimate LinkedIn Profile in Under an Hour* by Andrew Macarthy.

This is not the main reason I recommend LinkedIn to you, though. Indeed, if you are thinking about changing your career, your profile will probably not yet show the information that recruitment agencies are looking for. However, LinkedIn enables you to connect to people in your desired industry and profession and approach them directly. This can be a powerful tool.

I am regularly contacted on LinkedIn by people who want to get into legal or coaching careers and are looking for advice on how to go about it. I am often happy to advise or signpost them and many other people on LinkedIn will respond to such requests too. Some may ignore you, but this is part of any job hunt.

Go to LinkedIn, search for people who work in the profession, industry or company you want to work for and send them a personal message asking for advice. Some of them may even be willing to mentor you.

Here are a few tips for approaching people you do not know on LinkedIn:

- Don't just click the "connect" button. Send them a personal message.

- Keep the message short. This will make it much more likely that the recipient will read it and reply.

- Introduce yourself politely and share something personal, for example that you have a dream of getting into the same profession.

- Be specific about what you want from them, for example: *"I was wondering whether you have some advice for me about how to get into marketing, considering that my background so far has been solely in project management."*

Talk to a coach or career advisor

A coach will offer you a creative thinking space in which you can generate new ideas for finding your dream job. He will assist you in accessing your own resources and also hold you accountable for your actions. In addition, he will support you when struggling with any personal issues that are holding you back, such as lack of confidence, fears or procrastination.

If you are looking for specialist advice about career paths, CV writing, job requirements and market data, then a career advisor will be a better choice than a coach. Look for a career advisor who is specialised in the profession or industry that you are considering. She will share her expertise and may even have contacts that could help you.

Find a mentor

A great way to get into, or progress in, a career is to find a mentor who has already achieved what you are aspiring to do. A mentor is a person who is more experienced than you in the area that you want to develop. He or she will meet with you regularly to discuss your ambitions, strategies and progress. They can share with you a wealth of knowledge from their own experience.

If you do not yet know anybody who could be your mentor, you could approach someone via LinkedIn or another professional network. Be brave and daring, while also polite and respectful. I used to think that busy executives would regard such approaches as a nuisance. This may be true for some of them, but I also found executives who love to mentor because it gives them additional purpose. If you are holding back from asking others to mentor you, you are actually depriving them of an opportunity to create more meaning in their lives.

Start studying

If you already know that you will need additional skills or qualifications for your desired profession, you could enrol in a relevant course. As you are learning, you will find out more about your desired career and also create new connections. Additional skills and qualifications will also increase your chances of success with any of the routes I have covered here.

Work experience

Any kind of work experience in your desired career will increase your chances. Obviously, you will need to have time for this and if you are working full-time it may be difficult to organise. For this reason, this option will be most relevant to students or people out of work.

Having said that, for some careers there are volunteering opportunities that you could pursue alongside your existing job. A good example is the volunteering scheme of the Metropolitan Police in London, which gives members of the public the opportunity to support the police force in their spare time.

Chapter 24

Yes, but…

So you have done the exercises, you have a few ideas about finding a new career, but the big "BUT" kicks in. You think it is not really possible to find that fulfilling job, or at least not for you.

I have already discussed two typical objections in Chapter 2. Let's look at other objections you may have:

It is too late for me to change careers

Most of my clients come to me in their forties. Surprisingly, though, it is the younger ones who sometimes tell me that it is too late to change their careers. It's not. It never is. I retrained as a coach at 45, after 20 years in law and financial services.

I love working with clients in their forties because it is an excellent and exciting time to change the direction of our careers. If you allow me some bold and cheeky generalisations here, I'd put it this way: When we are in our twenties we often think we are so smart and know better than anybody else. In our thirties we are fully focused on establishing ourselves in our careers or building a family. In our forties we have done all that and suddenly ask ourselves: Is this all? There must be more! Why am I burnt out or dissatisfied?

I love the potential our forties and even fifties have in our life. By this age we have gained a lot of experience and still have a few decades ahead of us. We have proven ourselves and are better placed to know what we want. We may even have accumulated some assets that give us a financial cushion.

But change is possible at *all* ages. In Appendix 4 you will find a list of inspiring case studies of people who started completely new careers in their fifties to eighties! This includes the story of Andrea Peterson, who became a firefighter at age 66; Julie Kertesz, who became a stand-up comedian in her seventies; and Ress Fix, who started a career in television commercials in her eighties.

I have the deepest respect for all those amazing people who have started something new in their later years. I want to be like them: brave, adaptable and full of life until the very end. If these things are possible after the age of 60 and even in your eighties, just think about how much more you can create if you are only in your forties or even younger!

Don't buy into stories like "it's too late because…" They are simply beliefs that will kill your resourcefulness and will hold you back. Replace them with the question: *"How* can *I* do ….?" This is the question that creates new options for your life.

If you are dissatisfied with your job at any stage, then don't make this about your age. My question to you is whether you can afford to waste more years in a job you do not love. Can you afford the energy and joy it costs you? Maybe it has even cost you your health or a relationship? How much longer do you want to wait?

Most people have to work until their sixties or even seventies, so if you are in your thirties or forties that's far too long to stay in a job you do not enjoy. In fact, I believe that just a single year in a job you do not love is too much. There are some exceptions, of course; for example, if you are close to retirement and you do not want to lose out on your employer's company pension scheme, or if you need to maintain the job while you are creating new opportunities.

I often hear that employers do not want to hire mature staff. They want young people. Maybe that's true for certain jobs but these are probably not the ones you want to compete for anyway.

There is value in the experience that you have gained in your life and there are people out there who need that experience. This is different from the value that young people bring. There is no need to compete with them. For example, in professions such as coaching, therapy and consultancy, age is often an advantage. It gives you gravitas and credibility. You can also set up your own business where age does not matter because you are your own boss.

Employers are well advised to consider the value that mature employees can bring to their organisation. In any event, most western countries now prohibit unjustified age discrimination in all aspects of employment, including the recruitment process.

There are many people like me who were brave enough to break out of their job and create something new later in their life. It may be a different employer, a different work location, a different role at work or an entirely different career; it may even be setting up your own business. You have plenty of choices. Look out for people who have done this. Speak to them. Learn from them – and be truly open to the possibilities in your life.

Case study: Burn-out at 40

When James came to me, he was close to a breakdown from working for a large law firm. He was in his mid-forties, completely overworked, full of resentment for his job and with chest pain caused by the stress he was under. We explored his options and he very quickly realised that he had already made up his mind. He just had not been brave enough yet to accept his resolution.

When we discussed the options of staying in his job, asking for a new role or improving his self-management, he was very clear that he did not want to pursue any of them. He wanted to leave. When he came to this realisation in our first coaching session, he felt relieved and inspired. Two weeks later he had already handed in his notice, although his boss had made him various offers to tempt him to stay.

It was amazing to see how James livened up after he had handed in his notice. His mood improved, he started socialising and exercising again and was excited about his future – and the chest pain was gone.

James decided to train as a coach with a view to working with corporations to help them improve their levels of staff wellbeing and engagement. I know that he will be brilliant in this new role.

I do not have time to work on this

If you are one of those people who are completely drowned by the demands of their job, family and other commitments, then you may think that you simply do not have the time to work through the exercises in this book, research new jobs or careers and then go out to look for them.

If this is you, then I invite you to think again. This is your life. There is nothing more important than that. Your employers will only be loyal to you for as long as you are useful to them. Put yourself first. As you will have read in Chapter 4, I burnt myself out working on a deal for my employer which fell through just a few months after I eventually had to sign off sick. Do you really want to place your work demands above your wellbeing?

If you believe that you have to stay in your job to support your family, consider that you will have little to give to them if you burn out or are depressed about your work.

Understand your priorities and decide how much importance you want to give to your fulfilment in life and your wellbeing. If you do not create time for *your* priorities, you will always be swamped by the priorities of *others*.

If you are serious about your wellbeing, make time for your life planning and personal development. There are many ways in which you could do this; for example:

- go away for a weekend to think about the topics in this book at your leisure and without distractions
- get a coach to explore your desires and options
- block out regular hours in your calendar for reflective time
- book yourself into workshops about career and life planning
- talk to supportive friends and family members about your career planning

I need the money

Probably the most common reason why people are reluctant to look for career alternatives is money. They regard their monthly pay cheque as necessary to maintain their lifestyle, pay off debts or support their family. Before you put your dreams of a more fulfilling career aside for these reasons, have a think about how much money you really need.

When I landed my first legal job, I was amazed by the size of my first salary. It was more than I ever thought I would earn (admittedly my expectations were quite low!). From there on my salary rapidly increased every year until it reached well into six figures. Yet it never seemed enough. I raised my lifestyle at the same speed as my salary and somehow the money was always gone by the end of the month.

When I quit my job in financial services, my income dropped to a third of what it was at first. Strangely, it did not make a big impact on my lifestyle. Yes, I refrained from big ticket expenses for a while, but generally I still lived pretty well. This always amazes me. Money is so relative and often we do not really need all that cash that we are so keen to accumulate.

Exercise 12: How much money do you really need?

I encourage you to complete this exercise so that you understand how much money you really need. I am not necessarily suggesting that you compromise all the way down to your bottom line when looking for a new job, but understanding where your bottom line is will give you more options.

Take some time out to crunch numbers and answer the following questions:

	Life Style Level	List your cost items	Add up your cost items
A	Survival Level What are your regular essential costs? e.g.: • food • mortgage • rent • utility bills • insurances • hairdresser • public transport		Total of your items in Row A:

B	Adequate Level What are your regular fun and comfort expenses? e.g.: • eating out • going to the cinema • gym membership • dry cleaning • house cleaner		Total of your items in Rows A+B:
C	Comfort Level What is the monthly minimum budget that you want for extra expenses? e.g.: • holidays • buying clothing • house improvements • gadgets • entertaining		Total of your items in Rows A+B+C:

Now reflect on your list:

- Which of the three levels are you willing to live at during your time of transition?
- Which level once you have your new job?

If you now realise that you are willing to live on less money than you currently earn, what new options does this open up for you?

Let's face it, we all love having money, but nobody wants an income just for the sake of it. We want it for something that we get from it and that's different from person to person. It could be comfort, status, security, providing for your family, power, freedom, or to give back to people in need. Your reason may be one of those or something different.

The strange thing is that sometimes we cannot see how the job we have that provides us with all that money actually keeps us away from what we really want:

- You may want money to have more freedom, but your money and your possessions have become like a golden cage.
- You may want the money to provide for your family, but what your family needs much more is that you spend more time with them and that you are healthy and fulfilled.
- You may want money for security, but by burning yourself out at work you risk losing your health, friends, family and joy in life.

Whatever it is you gain from money, have a think about the price you may be paying for it and then reconsider how much money you really need. What would you gain in life by earning less money?

I love this classic Brazilian story which illustrates the point so well.

A wealthy businessman walks along a beach in a small Brazilian village. He stops to watch a fisherman pulling in his catch of the day and starts a conversation:

Businessman:	*How long did it take you to catch all that fish?*
Fisherman:	*Not very long.*
Businessman:	*Why did you not stay longer to catch more fish? It's early in the day.*
Fisherman:	*This is enough for me and my family.*
Businessman:	*What are you going to do for the rest of the day then?*
Fisherman:	*I am going home now to spend some time with my family, play with the kids and have a nap. In the evenings I usually hang around with my mates in the village. We have a drink, dance and play the guitar.*
Businessman:	*Listen, I am a successful businessman and would love to help you with some advice. If you were to stay out on the sea for longer and catch as many fish as you can, you would earn a lot more money.*
Fisherman:	*Why would I want to do that?*
Businessman:	*Well, with the additional money, you could buy a second boat and earn even more money. Soon you could have your own fleet of fishing boats.*
Fisherman:	*What good would that do to me?*
Businessman:	*You would earn even more money and eventually you could build your own fish cannery.*
Fisherman:	*What good would that do to me?*

Businessman:	*You could become incredibly rich like me. You could have other people doing all the work for you.*
Fisherman:	*What good would that do to me?*
Businessman:	*Eventually, you could retire and do all the things you love doing like going fishing, spending time with your family and going out with your friends.*
Fisherman:	*Isn't that what I am doing now?*

If you're earning money to be able to do something later in life, have a think about how you could have that thing already now, without having to wait until your retirement.

I need to provide for my family

This objection has some merit for many people. Of course, your family needs to have certain essentials such as a home, food on the table and education for your kids. All of this costs money.

As I alluded to in the previous section, though, your family also has other needs. They need you to be present, healthy, engaging and in good spirits. The financial needs of your family need to be balanced with their emotional needs. In Chapter 25, you will find the case study of Michael which shows how your family could suffer if you burn yourself out at work.

If you don't pay attention to the emotional needs of your family you could lose them. Your partner may leave you; your kids may come to resent you and it might even have a negative impact on their development. If today was your last day of your life, would you regret not having spent more time at the office or not having spent more time with your family?

So again, my question to you is how much money do you really need to support your family? How much more love and support could you give them if you had a less demanding job or if you simply came back home in better spirits?

Case study: Providing for the family

Paul was presented with an exciting career opportunity: becoming the Director of Marketing at a retail fashion company. This was a big step up from where he was in his career. The problem was that the new job was in Manchester while he and his family lived in London. His wife was not prepared to move to Manchester and Paul also agreed that it would be better for his kids to stay in their school in London. Paul still wanted the job, though, and was considering commuting. He was planning to stay three days in Manchester and then commute between cities on the other two working days. Paul came to me as a sounding board for his plan.

I asked Paul what was important to him about the job. He answered that it was money, status and intellectual challenges. When I asked which of the three was most important to him, he replied that it was the money. My next question was what made the money important to him. Paul answered that the money would help him provide better for his family. This answer showed me that his family was very high on his values list, maybe even at the very top. I then asked him how it would affect his family if he took on the job and commuted back and forward between London and Manchester.

Paul immediately got it. It was one of those lightbulb moments. He realised that his family would suffer from him being absent half of the week; and on the days he was in London, he would probably be far too stressed and tired to fully engage with them. Suddenly the choice was clear to him. He declined the job in Manchester because to him it

> was more important to support his family by being with them rather than through the additional income from the new job.
>
> As it happened, just a few weeks later Paul landed an equally good job in London.

It's too risky. What if I fail?

In most cases a career transition is undoubtedly risky. Yet this needs to be balanced against the disadvantages of staying in your current job. Some of the risks of staying in your job that could be relevant to your life are:

- living a life without joy

- losing your mental or physical health

- losing your loved ones

- living without purpose

- not fully utilising your potential

- having regrets later in your life

Our desire for certainty and security can hold us back from manifesting the things we really want in life. People often say that change only happens outside the comfort zone. Are you willing to take the risk?

There are a number of ways in which you can reduce the risks associated with a career transition:

- Start learning your new skills and gaining new qualifications outside your working hours and only leave your job when you have secured a new position in your new profession.

- If you are thinking about setting up a business, start developing it in your spare time and only drop your day job when you are certain the business is right for you and has a chance of success.

- Reduce your working hours or move to a part-time job to create time to work towards your new career or business. You can then gradually phase out your old career as your new one becomes more successful. This is what I did when I retrained as a life coach.

- You may be able to secure a leaving package from your old employer as part of a redundancy, compromise agreement or early retirement package. This could then cover your bills while you are working on creating your new career.

What if you do all of the above and you still fail?

Well, what is failure? You may have heard the expression that there is no failure, just learning. Without those things that we often define as failures, we would not be able to learn. Many successful business people suffered several bankruptcies in life before they finally became successful. We can only really have success if we accept all the perceived failures that happen along the way.

Are you willing to take a risk to create a fulfilling career? What will happen if you don't? Can you afford the risk of not taking action?

I'm not confident enough

We often think that we need to have confidence *before* we do something that is outside of our comfort zone. Yet confidence is the *result* of doing those things, not a *prerequisite*. The way we build up confidence is by being brave and doing things that are outside of our comfort zone.

You can build your confidence by taking small steps and cultivate a new habit of taking challenging actions. A coach can support you on this journey.

I don't know how to go about it

If you do not know how to find your dream job, don't worry. Focus on how to find support that will help you moving forwards. Read Chapter 26 for inspiration about how to get started.

I don't have the qualifications

It is true that most employers expect certain qualifications from job applicants. For some jobs they are even mandatory, such as doctors and lawyers.

There are, however, examples of many famous people who managed to become successful without academic qualifications. Here are just a few of them:

- **Tommy Hilfiger:** The American fashion designer performed poorly at school because of his dyslexia. He chose not to attend college and began to work in retail clothing shops.

- **Steve Jobs:** It's said that the founder of Apple had difficulty functioning in a traditional classroom, frequently misbehaved and was suspended from school several times. After graduating from high school, he enrolled in Reed College in Portland but dropped out after one semester.

- **Sir Richard Branson:** The founder of Virgin Atlantic Airways, Virgin Records, Virgin Mobile and other Virgin brands never completed high school and dropped out at 16 years of age. Not only that, but he was dyslexic and had poor academic performance.

- **Bill Gates:** The billionaire and co-founder of Microsoft dropped out of Harvard to focus on building his company.

He has been the world's richest man for 13 consecutive years.

- **George Eastman:** The founder of Kodak dropped out of school and took a job at age 14 as an office boy.
- **Ray Kroc:** The founder of McDonald's dropped out of high school as a teenager and became the top salesperson of a company selling plastic cups. The rest is history.

If you do not have the right qualifications, it may be more difficult to find employment but it is still possible in many professions. You will have to communicate the value you bring in different ways, for example through your passion, commitment, life experience and transferable skills.

You could also set up your own business where your academic records do not matter. Or you could, of course, obtain the qualifications, like former chemist Andrea Peterson who retrained as a firefighter at age 66. Read more inspiring case studies in Appendix 4.

What is your commitment?

You may have other objections, fears and doubts than those discussed in this chapter. That's OK. What really counts is how committed you are to creating a career that excites and fulfils you.

To do this you will have to step out of your comfort zone, do some deep soul-searching and then take action and accept some risks.

This is not for everybody. The majority of the population probably prefers to maintain their current work situation, even if it is unpleasant. At least you know what you're dealing with. Change comes with uncertainty and this scares many people.

You will have to balance the risk of a career change against the benefits that could come with it. Some of you will never be prepared to make the move, others (like me!) only after their situation has reached rock bottom. You do not have to wait that long, though.

How important is your fulfilment in life and your wellbeing to you? How much power do you want to give to your fears?

Chapter 25

Creating a healthy life balance

There is more to life than just work. You already know this.

In Chapter 6 I invited you to drop the concept of a "work-life balance" and instead see work as an enjoyable part of your life. You still need to balance your work with other parts of your life though, such as your family, wellbeing and hobbies.

What does life balance mean to you?

It is for you to decide what a healthy balance means to you. How much time and effort do you want to give to each area in your life? The answer will differ for each person. For example:

- having a relationship may not be important to you right now and you are quite happy to spend a lot of time at work

- your weekends may be sacred to you and you are not prepared to spend them working

- maybe you need to go out with friends at least twice a week to satisfy your need for socialising

- maybe a regular meditation or exercise regime is important to you

- you may want to balance your work with your spiritual journey

We are all different. The beauty of life is that we can decide what to create for ourselves.

There is only one obvious area which I advise you not to compromise on, and that is your wellbeing. Your physical and mental wellbeing are critical to your ability to function effectively and enjoy your life. If you neglect this area out of duty to your employer, work or family, you are in danger of damaging your health and depleting your resources to the extent that you are no longer able to serve the ones that you intended to help.

Case study: Maintaining balance

Michael is a client of mine who was struggling to balance the demands of his business, marriage and kids. He felt obliged to devote all his time and energy to those three areas in his life, but whatever he did he felt that his efforts were just not good enough. The needs of those around him seemed endless. He was craving some "me" time, like going to the gym or meeting friends, but felt too guilty satisfying his own needs because of a sense of responsibility for the people who depended on him.

When he came to me he had been neglecting his own needs for several years. He was burnt out, suffered from health issues and was on anti-depressants. It did not take long for him to understand that his strategy of devoting all his time and energy to others was not sustainable, and neither was it in the best interests of his business or family.

How effective could he really be as an overworked and stressed father and business owner? How much love and support could he give to his family when he was also resenting the burden they placed on him? And how much use would he be if he eventually burnt out and collapsed?

When I reflected his situation back to Michael, he understood that he would be able to give much more support to his family and colleagues if he took care of his own needs more; for example, taking regular time out alone, meditating, exercising and having fun with friends.

It's like they tell you on the plane: Put your own oxygen mask on first and then help others.

Exercise 13: Create Your Life Balance

Step 1: The Wheel of Life

*(You can download this and all other exercises from this book in a single document on the website **www.LoveYourJobBook.com**.)*

Let's take a basic snapshot of your current life balance. In the diagram below, rate each area in your life by giving it a value between:

10 (= complete satisfaction) and 0 (= complete disaster)

Mark your scoring on the diagram by connecting the numbers that match your scoring for the relevant segment. For example, if you score your satisfaction with your career as "5", connect the number 5s on each side of the Career segment. This creates a visual reflection of the way you feel about your life.

A perfectly fulfilled life would look like a full circle.

Your Wheel of Life

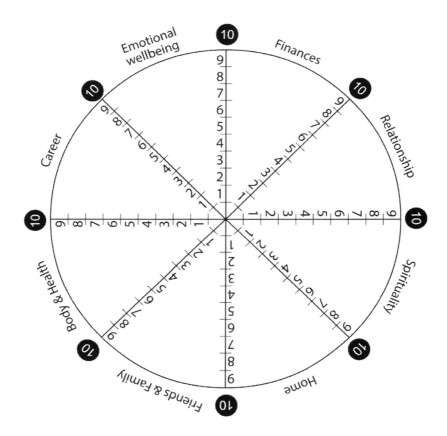

Diagram 4

Looking at your Wheel of Life, do you already see an imbalance that you would like to address? Have a think about the reasons for that imbalance. If you have focused your life mainly on work, it could be because you truly love making it the focus of your life. However, it could also be a substitute for other areas in your life that you have not managed to fulfil. For example, have you given up on the idea of finding a relationship and devoted your life to work because you no longer believe that you can find a lover?

In the next exercise you have an opportunity to explore what exactly needs to happen to bring your satisfaction to a 10 out of 10 in each section of the Wheel of Life.

You do not *need* to develop all areas in your Wheel of Life. Some of them may just not be that important to you. The ones that are critical to look after are your physical and mental wellbeing. Just for the sake of the exercise, however, I invite you to think about all segments in the Wheel of Life. You can then decide which ones to follow up with actions.

Step 2: Define your Life Goals

The table below lists all eight areas from the Wheel of Life that you completed in the previous exercise. In this step, you can define for each area what exactly would be required to bring your satisfaction to a 10 out of 10.

This works best if you are very specific, because if you do not define what exactly you want in life it will be difficult for you to create a success strategy for achieving those things. You may also miss the joy of celebrating your success. How can you know that you have reached your goals if you never defined them?

When you write down your goals, make them meaningful and measurable by using the SMART criteria:

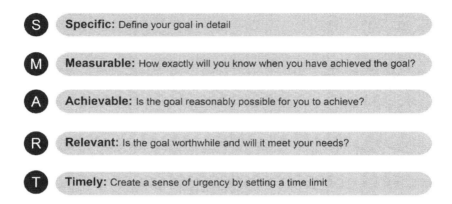

Here are a few examples that show how vague goals can be turned into SMART ones:

Vague goal	SMART goal
I want to become thinner	I want to reduce my weight to 75Kg at 14% body fat by 1 January 2018
I want more friends	By the end of 2017, I want to have three additional close friends who I see at least once every week
I want to run a successful business	I want to own a wine shop in Brighton that generates £50,000 in annual profits by 2020.

Get the idea? The more specific you are, the better you will know what you have to do and when you have achieved your goal.

Now over to you. Complete the table below with your SMART

goals for each area of your life that would bring your satisfaction in that area to a 10 out of 10:

*(You can download this and all other exercises from this book in a single document on the website **www.LoveYourJobBook.com**.)*

Your life area	What would make this a 10 out of 10? (Be specific using SMART goals)
Career	
Friends & Family	
Relationship	

Finance	
Home	
Spirituality	
Emotional Wellbeing	
Body & Health	
Other areas that are important to you	

Step 3: Balance your life

*(You can download this and all other exercises from this book in a single document on the website **www.LoveYourJobBook.com**.)*

Now that you have established your level of satisfaction in each area of your life and identified what you feel is missing, consider what, if anything, you need to change about your work life to create a more satisfying and healthier balance with the other areas in your life. Consider both what *needs* to change and what you are *willing* to change.

Write down what adjustments you want to make in your life. Once again I am asking you to be specific using the SMART criteria. For example, instead of writing that you want to leave work at a reasonable hour, state at what time, or within which time window, you want to leave work and on what days of the week.

Over to you!

What needs to change in your life balance?

_____

_____

_____

_____

_____

What are you willing to change?

_____

_____

_____

_____

_____

What are you deciding now to change, and by when?

_____

_____

_____

_____

_____

The time issue

In Western society we never seem to have time. Despite having so many more machines and technology available to make our life easier, we never seem to have enough time to do all the things in life that we want to pursue.

You may have come up with a number of inspiring goals in the Wheel of Life exercise above, but now ask yourself how to find the time to work on them. How about starting with working on just one area at a time? We do not want this to create another layer of stress in your life.

I mentioned in a number of places in this book that we need to be clear about our priorities and make time for them. If we do not consciously create time for those things that are important to us, we risk being stuck on a treadmill that leaves us dissatisfied and restricts our personal growth.

Let's look at a few ways in which you could create space in your life for things that are important to you:

- **Leaving work on time:** You could leave work on time at least on a few days each week. If you find it difficult to be disciplined about this, book yourself on a regular course, sport activity or appointment with a trainer or coach. Once you have made a commitment to somebody else, you are more likely to make it and your colleagues will hopefully understand.

- **Take your lunch hour:** I am a firm believer in taking a full hour for lunch every day, ideally outside your office. Have a healthy lunch, meet a friend, meditate, go for a walk or read a fun book. You will return replenished and probably be more productive.

- **Keep your weekends free of work:** This may be difficult for some of you but have a think where you want to set your boundaries. If you don't set and communicate them, it's far more likely that work will encroach into your private space.

- **Leave work at the office:** If you bring work back home, it will reduce your well-deserved recovery time and you will be less available for your friends and family.

- **Take mobile phone breaks:** Switch off your work mobile or leave it at home when you are outside work. At the very least, resist checking your messages all the time. You could set up a rule that you will only check them once or twice each evening or weekend at specific times.

- **Ask for flexible working hours:** More and more employers allow them now. This will enable you to plan your work hours around other important items in your life, such as attending a yoga class, going to the doctor, running errands or seeing your kids performing in a school play.

- **Say "no" more often:** If your employer is understaffed, why should you make up for it by sacrificing your evenings and weekends? It's OK when this happens occasionally, but if it becomes a constant feature of your work life decide on your boundaries and clearly communicate them.

- **Block out time:** You could block out time at work when you make yourself unavailable to others so that you can work on matters that are important to you, such as developing your professional skills or creating a new business strategy. Turn off the internet, put your phone on forwarding or go somewhere where nobody will find you for an hour.

- **Increase your efficiency:** You could learn how to work more efficiently. If this is of interest, I recommend the book *Eat That Frog* by Brian Tracy, which is packed with simple ideas to work more effectively. But be aware: unless you then prioritise what is important to you, you may find that all the efficiencies you create are immediately absorbed by new demands from the people around you.

- **Diarise fun events:** I find that if I do not plan for holidays, parties at my place and other social events well in advance, they just don't happen. At the beginning of each year, I decide how many holidays I want to take and block them in my diary so that no client can book them. I also decide on how many parties I want to throw in the year and diarise them as well.

- **Identify time leeches:** It's worth recording your activities for a week to see how exactly you spend your time. Many people claim to be busy, but then spend hours watching TV, playing games, chatting on social media or browsing the internet. There is nothing wrong with these activities, but if you are looking to free up more time, these could be areas where you might be able to easily win an hour or so each day.

Now you know what you want to do to improve your life balance. The next step is action. Keep up the momentum! Plan now when and how you will do what you have decided on – and then do it. Tell others about your goals so that they can hold you accountable. Get a coach to keep you on track and support you through the challenges on your journey.

Part 5

Taking action

In this part of the book:

- ✓ You will bring all key parts of your work together in one Life Plan

- ✓ You will explore what to do next to continue your journey to job satisfaction

- ✓ You will explore who can support you on this journey

- ✓ You will find tips for choosing a personal coach

Chapter 26

What to do next

You have nearly finished reading this book and I hope that you have completed all of the exercises. If you have, I trust you will have gained more clarity about your desires and options in relation to your job and career.

What else can you do to maximise the benefits from this book?

Bring it all together

In Appendix 2 you will find a template that allows you to summarise your life vision by bringing the following together in one document called **"Life Plan"**:

- your personal mission statement from Chapter 8;
- your highest personal values from Chapter 7;
- your BEs, DOs and HAVEs from Chapter 8; and
- your life goals and action lists from Chapter 25.

Having it all at hand in one document will make it easier for you to keep your work present and to review it regularly.

Take action!

This step is important: If you do not take action, then reading this book was just an intellectual exercise. You purchased this book and invested your time working through its exercises to improve your job satisfaction. You were looking for fulfilment, inspiration and excitement – and you can have it all. You just need to follow through on the actions that you decided on as you were completing the exercises.

Review your values, missions and action plans regularly

In Chapter 8 I explained the importance of keeping your values and mission alive by revisiting them regularly. If you have not yet done so, diarise review points of your Life Plan, at least annually. I also recommend that you revisit your specific actions from your Life Plan once a month to check whether you are on track with them. If you are behind, what are the reasons? Is your plan not exciting enough? Make adjustments as necessary and explore any doubts or fears that may be holding you back.

Go public

A great way to ensure that you follow through on your actions is to tell others about your commitments. They will keep asking you how you are doing, and who wants to admit that they did not follow through as they said they would?

Get support

It's likely that you already have people in your network who can help with advice, listening, brainstorming or simply holding you accountable to your goals.

Support can come from many places. Let's have a look at some options:

- **Trusted friends and family members:** Be aware though; only share when you know that they are truly supportive! Don't talk to your family if they are the sort of people who are always negative, want you to live their values or otherwise want to keep you in your place.

- **Your manager or colleagues**: Again, consider whether you can trust them.

- **Your HR department:** You will probably only want to speak to them if you are looking for career options at your current company.

- **A mentor:** A mentor is a person who is more experienced and knowledgeable than you in an area that you would like to grow in. When you choose a mentor, you may want to select one who has been successful in the industry you are interested in or has otherwise achieved something that you aspire to. I recommend you choose a mentor at another company if you are considering leaving your employment so that you can speak to him or her freely.

- **Professional support:** This could be a coach or career advisor.

- **Role models:** This could be somebody you know, or somebody you don't know personally but admire. If you do not know them you could still ask them for help. See Chapter 23 where I talk about approaching people you do not know via LinkedIn. Otherwise you could read about them and try to model their way to success based on the information you find out about them.

Exercise 14: Who do you know?

*(You can download this and all other exercises from this book in a single document on the website **www.LoveYourJobBook.com**.)*

Write down below the names of people who could help you on your journey to creating excitement and fulfilment in your career:

_____

_____

_____

_____

_____

Get a coach

You can make your journey a lot easier and faster if you hire a personal coach. It's a bit like personal training. You will probably never push yourself as hard or effectively as a personal trainer would. You create better and faster results with the support of a trainer who understands your unique situation and designs a bespoke programme just for you, providing advice, setting challenges and holding you accountable along the way. It's the same with personal coaching.

Coaching is an investment in your life and I value it so much that I will always want to have my own coach. Just like an athlete continues to train and improve his performance after a win, I want to continue my own journey to what I call Masterful Living®.

Here are a few tips for finding a coach:

- Does she or he hold a diploma or other coaching qualification which is accredited by the International Coach Federation (ICF)?

- Is she or he personally accredited by the International Coach Federation (ICF)?

- Can she or he demonstrate a specialisation in the area in which you want to be coached?

- Does she or he have testimonials from satisfied clients?

- Is she or he a performance coach (a coach who helps you explore options and strategies for getting from A to B) or a transformational coach (who can also do deeper work, for example by asking who you need to be to get from A to B)?

- Have you checked for how long she or he has been in the coaching business?

- Does she or he have any professional experience outside coaching that could be useful in the coaching relationship?

- Have you had a trial session and established that the chemistry between you is right?

- Does she or he listen to you instead of just talking about herself or himself?

Download the free bonus material

You will find various free materials on the website **www. LoveYourJob.com**. They include a downloadable version of all the exercises in this book so that you can print them out and complete them as often as you like.

On that website you can also download my eBook *The 10 Basics of Masterful Living*® that will provide you with inspiration for your personal growth in all areas of your life.

Surround yourself with like-minded people

The rate of your personal growth will be affected by the company you keep. Have you ever been in a situation where you told a friend about an idea that you were excited about and he responded with cynicism, jokes or disinterest? Did it knock down your enthusiasm? Maybe you even felt silly about your dream after you shared it.

On the other hand, imagine if you were surrounded by ambitious people who share your interest in personal growth and inspire you with their achievements. You support and learn from each other, share experiences and celebrate success. Can you see how this would reinforce your commitment and keep you on track?

Or think even bigger and surround yourself with people who have already created the success you are after. You can learn from them and get inspiration or even mentoring. You can model their success. How powerful would that be!

I am not suggesting that you get rid of your current social network. As with everything, just become aware of your surroundings, create a balance if necessary and do what is required to build the most supporting environment for your journey of creating a job you love.

Chapter 27

Conclusion

Congratulations! You are at the end of this book. If you have completed all the exercises, you will have:

- established your core values;

- created an inspiring vision for your life;

- explored the factors that will improve your job satisfaction; and

- decided on actions to improve your life balance.

You now have all the tools you need to create an inspiring and exciting career. Now it's over to you to implement your plan, take action and enjoy your chosen job.

I would love to hear your success stories. There is a real person behind this book who is interested in hearing from you. Your stories will not only increase my sense of purpose, they will also help me to grow and further refine my methodologies so that I can provide more value to my clients and readers.

You can contact me at: **info@hansschumann.com**

I wish you a life full of inspiring challenges, exciting successes and a deep love for what you do.

Hans Schumann

The Masterful Living® Coach

Appendix I

The Demartini Value Determination Process®

Printed by permission of the Demartini Institute

For more information, please visit: **www.drdemartini.com** or read the book, *The Values Factor - The Secret to Creating an Inspired and Fulfilling Life* by Dr John Demartini, a book which changed my life.

You can also take this test online at www.drdemartini.com/values

Determine your values, step by step

The Demartini Value Determination Process® was developed by Dr John Demartini, author, educator, leadership and performance specialist. This is a multi-step process in which you keep refining your answers until your hierarchy of values finally emerges with crystal clarity.

Step One:

Answer the following 13 questions

1. How do you fill your personal space?

Have you ever noticed how things that are really not important to you go into the trash, the attic, or the storage closet? By contrast, you keep the things that are important to you where you can see them, either at home or at work.

What does your life demonstrate through your space? When you look around your home or office, do you see family photos, sports trophies, business awards, books? Do you see beautiful objects, comfortable furniture for friends to sit on, or souvenirs of favorite places you've visited? Perhaps your space is full of games, puzzles, DVDs, CDs, or other forms of entertainment. Whatever you see around you is a very strong clue as to what you value most.

What 3 things fill your space?

_____

_____

_____

_____

_____

2. How do you spend your time?

Here's something you can count on: people always make time for things that are really important to them and run out of time for things that aren't. Even though people usually say, "I don't have time for what really I want to do," the truth is that they are too busy doing what is truly most important to them. And what they think they want to be doing isn't really what's most important. You always find time for things that are really important to you. Somehow, you figure it out.

So how do you spend your time? I personally spend my days researching, writing, teaching, and traveling. Those are my four highest values. I always find time for doing them. And I almost never find time for cooking, driving, and doing domestic things, which are low on my list of values. How you spend your time tells you what matters to you most.

In which three ways do you spend your time?

_____

_____

_____

_____

_____

3. How do you spend your energy?

You always have energy for things that inspire you – the things you value most. You run out of energy for things that don't. Things that are low among your values drain you; things that are high among your values energize you. In fact, when you are doing something that you value highly, you have more energy at the end of the day than when you started because you're doing something that you love and are inspired by. So how do you spend your energy – and where do you get your energy?

In which three ways do you spend your energy and where do you feel energized?

_____

_____

_____

_____

_____

4. How do you spend your money?

Again, you always find money for things that are valuable to you, but you never want to part with your money for things that are not important to you. So your choices about spending money tell you a great deal about what you value most. Now, at this point, you might be noticing some overlap: some similarities between what you fill your space with and how you spend your time, energy, and money. That is healthy. It means that you have already aligned a lot of your values, goals, and daily activities. If you notice a lot of divergence between the answers to these first four questions, you might benefit from bringing your values and goals into deeper alignment.

In which three ways do you spend your money?

_____

_____

_____

_____

_____

5. Where do you have the most order and organization?

We tend to bring order and organization to things that are important to us and to allow chaos and disorder with things that are low on our values. So look at where you have the greatest order and organization in your life, and you'll have a good sense of what matters most to you. In my case, I see the most order and organization in my research and teaching materials, and in my itinerary for traveling. This helps me see that my values involve research, writing, teaching, and travel.

In which three areas are you most organized?

_____

_____

_____

_____

_____

6. Where are you most reliable, disciplined, and focused?

You never have to be reminded from the outside to do the things that you value the most. You are inspired from within to do those things and so you do them. Look at the activities, relationships, and goals for which you are disciplined, reliable, and focused – the things that nobody has to get you up to do. For me, again, that's researching, writing, travel, speaking, and teaching. I love those things!

In which three activities and areas are you most reliable, disciplined and focused?

_____

_____

_____

_____

_____

7. What do you think about, and what is your most dominant thought?

I'm not talking about the negative self-thought or the things that distract you. I'm not talking about the fantasies, "shoulds" or "oughts." I'm talking about your most common thoughts about how you want your life–thoughts that you show slow or steady evidence of actually bringing to fruition.

What are your three most dominant thoughts?

_____

_____

_____

_____

_____

8. What do you visualize and realize?

Again, I'm not talking about fantasies. I'm asking what you visualize for your life that is slowly but surely coming true. In my case, I visualize travelling the world and setting foot in every country on the face of the Earth. That is what I visualize. And that is what I am realizing. So what are you visualizing and realizing?

What are the three ways you visualize your life?

_____

_____

_____

_____

_____

9. What is your internal dialogue?

What do you keep talking to yourself about the most? I am not asking about negative self-talk or self-aggrandizement. I want you to think of your preoccupation with what you desire most–intentions that actually seem to be coming true and showing some fruits.

What are the three things that you have internal dialogues about?

_____

_____

_____

_____

_____

10. What do you talk about in social settings?

Okay, now here's a clue that you'll probably notice for other people as well as yourself. What are the topics that you keep wanting to bring into the conversation that nobody has to remind you to talk about? What subjects turn you into an instant extrovert?

Whether your 'baseline' personality is extrovert or introvert, you've probably noticed that there are topics that immediately bring you to life and start you talking and others that turn you into an introvert who has nothing to say – or make you want to change the subject. You can use this same insight to analyze other people's values. If you go up to somebody and they ask you about your kids, that means their kids are important to them. If they say, "How's business?" they value business. If they ask, "Are you seeing anyone new?", then relationships matter to them. Topics that attract you are a key to what you value.

What are the three things that you speak about in social settings?

_____

_____

_____

_____

_____

11. What inspires you?

What inspires you now? What has inspired you in the past? What is common to the people who inspire you? Figuring out what inspires you most reveals what you value most.

What are the three things that inspire you the most?

_____

_____

_____

_____

_____

12. What are the most consistent long-term goals that you set?

What are the three long-term goals that you have focused on that you are bringing into reality? Again, I'm not talking about the fantasies that nothing is happening with. I want the dreams you are bringing into reality slowly but surely, the dreams that have been dominating your mind and your thoughts for a time – the dreams that you are bringing into daily life, step by step by step.

What are the three most consistent long-term goals that you have set?

_____

_____

_____

_____

13. What do you love to learn and read about most?

What are the three most common topics you love learning or reading about most? What three topics can you stay focused on and love learning about without distraction.

What are the three things you love to learn and read about?

_____

_____

_____

StepTwo:

Identify the Answers That Repeat Most Often

Once you've written down three answers for each of the 13 questions, you'll see that among your 39 answers, there is a certain amount of repetition – perhaps even a lot of repetition. You may be expressing the same kinds of value in different ways – for example, "spending time with people I like," "having a drink with the folks from work," "going out to eat with my friends" – but if you look closely, you can see some patterns begin to emerge.

So look at the answer that is most often repeated and write beside it the number of how often it repeats. Then find the second most frequent answer, then the third, and so on, until you have ranked every single answer. This gives you a good primary indicator of what your highest values are. You can even start making decisions based on this initial hierarchy of values – and you can see how your life is already demonstrating your commitment to these values.

Appendix 2

Your Life Plan

My personal mission in one paragraph
My core values
1.
2.
3.

My BEs, DOs and HAVEs

BE (what I will be):

DO (what I will do):

HAVE (what I will have):

My life goals		
Life segment	My goals	By when?
Career		
Friends & Family		
Relationship		
Finance		
Home		

Spirituality		
Emotional Wellbeing		
Health & Body		
Other areas that are important to you		

Appendix 3

Transferable skills

There are countless transferable skills and this list only shows a few examples. Have a read through it and circle the ones you believe you are good at. Once you have gone through them all, you will get the idea and may be able to identify additional skills that you have.

Administering medication

Administration (office/processes)

Advising

Analysing data

Analysing problems

Articulating issues

Assembling equipment

Auditing data or processes

Being artistic/creative

Brainstorming

Budgeting

Building new businesses

Buildings things

Business management

Calculating data

Canning or preserving

Caring for others

Categorising records

Challenging people

Checking for accuracy

Cleaning

Coaching

Collaborating ideas

Collecting items

Communicating

Comparing facts or results

Compiling statistics

Comprehending books or ideas

Conducting interviews

Conducting meetings

Conflict resolution

Confronting other people

Constructing

Consulting

Cooking

Copywriting

Counselling people

Creating communities

Creating ideas or solutions

Creating new procedures

Creating presentations

Creating software

Creating spreadsheets

Creative thinking

Critical thinking

Customer service

Dealing with complaints

Decision-making

Defining performance standards

Delegating

Demonstrating

Designing systems

Developing and maintaining standards

Developing plans for projects

Diplomacy

Displaying art

Distributing products

Dramatising ideas

Editing

Effective listening

Encouraging people

Enforcing rules

Entertaining

Envisioning solutions or ideas

Estimating project workload

Evaluating

Event management

Expressing feelings

Expressing ideas

Extracting information

Filing records

Filming

Finding missing information

First aid

Following directions

Fundraising

Gardening

Gathering information

Generating accounts

Goal setting

Good with my hands

Hosting events

Human resource management

Identifying problems

Illustrating

Imagining innovative solutions

Information management

Initiating

Inspecting buildings

Inspecting equipment

Instructing others

Interacting with people

Interpreting languages

Interviewing

Inventing products/ideas

Investigating

Joking

Keeping financial records

Leading organisations

Leading teams

Lobbying

Locating answers or
information

Logical thinking

Maintaining accurate records

Maintaining discipline

Maintaining files

Maintenance of equipment or
processes

Making a household budget

Making important decisions

Managing finances

Managing money

Managing people

Managing projects

Marketing

Measuring boundaries

Mediating between people

Medical assistance

Meeting deadlines

Meeting new people

Meeting the public

Mentoring

Motivating others

Multi-tasking

Navigating politics

Negotiating

Networking

Observing and inspecting

Operating computers

Operating tools and machinery

Operating vehicles

Organising events

Organising files

Organising rooms or physical belongings

Organising tasks

Painting

Persuading

Planning

Planning meetings

Planning organisational needs

Plumbing

Preaching

Predicting future trends

Preparing written documents

Prioritising

Promoting events

Proofreading

Proposal writing

Proposing ideas

Providing customer service

Public relations

Publishing

Questioning others

Reading

Recognising problems

Recruiting

Regulating rules

Rehabilitating people

Relating to others

Remembering information

Repairing

Reporting data

Researching

Running meetings

Screening calls

Selling ideas

Selling products or services

Serving people

Setting performance standards

Sharing information

Sketching charts or diagrams

Sketching pictures

Solving problems

Speaking a foreign language

Speaking in public

Storytelling

Strategic thinking

Suggesting courses of action

Summarising data or problems

Supervising employees

Taking decisive action

Taking initiative

Taking inventory

Teaching

Team building

Team working

Technical design

Technical support

Technology

Thinking logically

Time management

Time-keeping

Tracking personal finances

Training

Translating

Typing

Updating files

Using complex equipment

Using computers

Word processing

Working with statistics

Writing clearly and concisely

Writing communications

Writing letters, papers, or
proposals

Appendix 4

Real-life examples of career changes in later life

The people mentioned in the following case studies are not personally known to me. The case studies are based on facts that were reported in public sources.

1. Making travelling your business

Silvana Clark (56) had been a writer and professional speaker and her husband Alan (59) a trainer of school bus drivers. To finance their ambition of travelling, the couple offered their services to Soles4Souls, a charity which provides footwear for poor and homeless people in the United States. They proposed that if Soles4Souls would buy them an RV, they'd drive it around the country, giving free shoes to the needy and promoting the organisation. Soles4Souls accepted and the Clarkes became their brand ambassadors. After travelling for Soles4Souls to 42 states over 19 months, the Clarkes accepted employment by Avon Care to drive around the country and help the company recruit representatives.

2. From building contractor to tutor placement

Barry Duckworth worked as a licensed general building contractor for 30 years, but when he was 59 he decided to look for a new career where he could be "a kinder person". He started his own tutor-placement business, matching kids with tutors who come to their homes.

3. From IT to cooking

After Maralee DeMark retired from her job as an information technology manager at age 55, she was ready for something new. She and her sister Diane DeMark (66), who had retired 10 years earlier, both loved to cook and entertain. They opened the Two Sisters Market Cafe in Terrell, N.C., which features locally grown organic cuisine.

4. A firefighter at age 66

Andrea Peterson, a former medical transcriptionist, fulfilled her childhood dream in her 60s. She wanted to be a firefighter, but her family talked her out of it when she was young. Andrea was 66 years old when she received her firefighter certification. She then started working at her New England village's fire department while also mentoring other women who want to become firefighters.

5. Graduating at age 69

At the age of 65, life-long entrepreneur Norm Smith looked for a new challenge. He sold his company that made plastic disposable medical containers, and applied for optometry courses at 17 colleges. Only one college replied and then accepted him as a student. Norm graduated at the age of 69 and set up his own optometry business.

6. Stand-up comedian at age 70

After her husband left her when she was 70, former chemist Julie Kertsz moved to London. She became a storyteller and later went to a stand-up comedy workshop. Now she performs stand-up comedy almost every week and her audience loves her. She also won a Toastmasters International gold award as an advanced communicator.

7. From car park to kitchen

After he took early retirement from his job as a car park manager at age 59, Frank Finlay became a teacher of horticulture at a technical college. When he was 62, he undertook another career change and started preparing breakfasts six mornings a week at the inn of a friend of his. He had enjoyed doing something different and completed a cookery course because "it's always handy to have a qualification".

8. Graphic design career at age 62

Alice Longworth had a full-time position in fundraising support, a role that she had been feeling was a poor fit for her interests and skills. She began taking graphic design classes and at age 62 became a graphic designer and communications coordinator for a church.

9. From redundancy to blogging

When Kay Roseland was made redundant in her 60s, she looked at this as an opportunity to start something new. She obtained two certifications in social media and created her own blog called Shareology. At age 64, Kay was hired to blog for software company Infor. She also mentors her boss, the vice president of product management, on using social media.

10. TV commercials at age 80

After retiring as a schoolteacher, Ress Fix enrolled in two commercial training courses. After that she got an agent and started her second career in television commercials at the age of 80. She featured in many TV commercials and magazine advertisements.

Printed in Great Britain
by Amazon